The Learning-Centered Kindergarten

This book is dedicated to my dad, James L. Cook, who was not only a wonderful role model, but an amazing teacher of how to live a full and productive life. His love and support were constant, his actions always honest. His heart always provided more than was expected or deserved by the ones he loved. We often discussed my ambition to write a book . . .

Look, Dad, I finally did it! I know you would be proud.

The Learning-Centered Kindergarten

10 Keys to Success for Standards-Based Classrooms

Shari Y. Ehly

CORWIN PRESS

A SAGE Company

For information:

Corwin Press
A SAGE Company
2455 Teller Road
Thousand Oaks, California 91320
www.corwinpress.com

SAGE Ltd.
1 Oliver's Yard
55 City Road
London, EC1Y 1SP
United Kingdom

SAGE India Pvt. Ltd.
B 1/I 1 Mohan Cooperative
   Industrial Area
Mathura Road, New Delhi 110 044
India

SAGE Asia-Pacific Pte. Ltd.
33 Pekin Street #02-01
Far East Square
Singapore 048763

Printed in the United States of America

Library of Congress Cataloging-in-Publication Data

Ehly, Shari Y.
  The learning-centered kindergarten : 10 keys to success for standards-based class-rooms / Shari Y. Ehly.
     p. cm.
  Includes bibliographical references and index.
  ISBN 978-1-4129-5546-1 (cloth : acid-free paper)
  ISBN 978-1-4129-5547-8 (pbk. : acid-free paper)
  1. Kindergarten—Methods and manuals.   2. Learning.   3. Teaching.   I. Title.

LB1169.E35 2009
372.21'8—dc22   2008004881

This book is printed on acid-free paper.

08   09   10   11   10   9   8   7   6   5   4   3   2   1

Acquisitions Editor:	Stacy Wagner
Managing Editor:	Jessica Allan
Editorial Assistant:	Joanna Coelho
Production Editor:	Appingo Publishing Services
Cover Designer:	Scott Van Atta

Contents

Foreword

Although kindergarten has been thoroughly blended into the U.S. public school system for more than fifty years, it has many features that set it apart from other elementary school grade levels. Seefeldt and Wasik (2002) describe kindergarten as "a special and unique place for children under the age of six" (p. 17) and contend that "the philosophy of valuing, treasuring, and protecting young children's right to their childhood makes today's kindergartens, like those of the past, a paradise of childhood" (Seefeldt & Wasik, 2002, p. 17). In the U.S. today, however, this understanding of kindergarten as a learning environment designed to serve the unique learning needs of young children is presently being challenged.

The No Child Left Behind Act of 2001 (NCLB) mandated the implementation of statewide accountability systems comprised of challenging state standards in reading and mathematics and annual testing to assess mastery of those standards for all public school students in grades three through eight. Although the primary grades and kindergarten were not included in NCLB legislation, concerns about preparing children to enter third grade with the foundational skills necessary to achieve acceptable test scores has caused a phenomenon Hatch refers to as "accountability shovedown" (Hatch, 2002, p. 457): In many states, the NCLB-driven emphasis on student mastery of a predetermined set of academic concepts and skills that characterizes the upper grades has been shoved down through the primary grades and all the way into kindergarten. Now, in addition to providing learning experiences that support the development of the whole child, kindergarten teachers are also held accountable for guiding their students towards mastery of the academic skills and content presented in their state's standards.

I recently studied how veteran kindergarten teachers were managing these new challenges. Participants in the study agreed that kindergarten had changed dramatically since the implementation of NCLB. But when I compared my detailed observations of these teachers' practices with their descriptions and recollections of their experiences in previous years, it seemed that their students' day-to-day classroom lives had not changed substantially

Despite the new expectations currently reshaping kindergarten, participants in the study found ways to continue using many of their tried-and-true instructional materials, curriculum units, projects, activities, books, and practices. Their students still go to learning centers and write in journals, still wiggle restlessly on their mats during rest time, and play together in the housekeeping center during free choice time. In these classrooms, it looks like kindergarten business as usual.

I discovered what has changed dramatically as a result of NCLB-driven policies and expectations is the behind-the-scenes complexity involved in teaching kindergarten. Years ago, teachers simply made use of the generous instructional and curricular latitude freely available to them and developed units of study offering learning experiences they believed would be beneficial to the children's growth across all developmental domains. Those days are gone. Now, kindergarten teachers need to be strategic, to seek out and lay claim to pockets of flexibility, and to identify and act on any available opportunities for customization and modification in order to create a kindergarten environment that will meet their students' learning needs. The kindergarten classrooms in my study looked and felt the same as they always have, but that continuity and stability came as a result of these teachers' tremendous initiative, dedication, and creativity.

Professional judgment was the key to these teachers' success in managing the current challenge of meeting the developmental needs of their students while satisfying the state mandates and district requirements. The participants of this study used their professional judgment tactically to claim the right to teach the standards in their own ways, to carve out free time and safe spaces to protect and facilitate their students' development, and to give themselves permission to do what they believed to be best for their kindergartners.

This useful book will help all kindergarten teachers—preservice, novice, and experienced—learn to use their professional judgment to help them succeed in meeting the challenges and demands of twenty-first-century classrooms. Shari Y. Ehly, an experienced kindergarten teacher, school administrator, and mentor, shares ten keys to success that will enable kindergarten teachers to maintain their dedication to meeting the needs of all learners in their classrooms, align their practices with today's expectations, and prepare themselves for professional success in the kindergartens of tomorrow.

Shari Y. Ehly's unique focus on the creation of *learning-centered* kindergartens brings together the established developmental kindergarten knowledge base, the current research on standards-based best practices in elementary school settings, and the newest findings on human learning to form a principled, practical, and effective approach to kindergarten teaching that will guide teachers in improving their classroom practices and maximizing their students' success. A classroom-friendly guide that links research and theory to practice, this book offers concrete, specific strategies that kindergarten teachers will be able to implement in their classrooms immediately.

Today's kindergarten teachers work in professional environments characterized by intense pressure to succeed and by uncertainty, ambiguity, and rapid change. Practicing professionals will benefit tremendously from *The Learning-Centered Kindergarten: 10 Keys to Success for Standards-Based Classrooms*, a book expressly designed to offer them support and guidance as they navigate the difficult circumstances currently confronting kindergarten teachers. Neither too broad to be useful nor too comprehensive and detailed to be applied easily, this book is both substantive and practical, and offers valuable hands-on advice drawn directly from the classroom experiences of a successful kindergarten practitioner.

My wish for all teachers—especially those who teach kindergarten like I did—is that they will find a wise, realistic, generous colleague at their school site: a mentor who will help them succeed in keeping their focus on the students' learning despite the challenges they face; a friend to remind them of the great joy and satisfaction that are the rewards of effective teaching; a "fairy godmother" ready to offer encouragement, guidance, and support as needed. Thanks to *The Learning-Centered Kindergarten: 10 Keys to Success for Standards-Based Classrooms,* my wish is coming true at last. Shari Y. Ehly's professional experience and knowledge base, her gentle humor and unflagging optimism, and her confidence in teachers' ability to delight in the possibilities that unfold when they take risks, try something new, and trust their students to be engaged, eager learners are now readily available to every kindergarten teacher. Enjoy!

Dr. Lisa S. Goldstein
Associate Professor and Director
Early Childhood Teacher Education
The University of Texas at Austin

Preface

In the summer of 1999, I was a kindergarten teacher who, after a much extended break from academia, decided to return to graduate school to earn a master's degree in curriculum and instruction. It was my extreme good fortune to have enrolled into the Curriculum Theory class of Lisa S. Goldstein, PhD, at the University of Texas. Her exquisite teaching provided thoughtful and challenging exploration into her students' values, teaching practices, and philosophies. Her insightful instruction guided us, as educators, to view the world through different lenses and, more importantly, to grow as professionals. The questions she posed in class related directly to all of us in very different, but very personal, ways. She always listened and validated our positions, but also wanted us to see things from different points of view.

A friendship grew from that class which resulted in long conversations about developmentally appropriate practices, parents, administrators, how the standards are changing kindergarten, and much, much more. Through the years, I changed career positions from kindergarten teacher to primary grade math coach, from instructional specialist to assistant principal. While my philosophies and passion for teaching remained constant, my view of the world changed. As a kindergarten teacher, my focus was upon just the students in *my* classroom, but as an administrator, I now must be concerned about the quality of learning experiences over extended time for each child at my campus. This book is a product of that friendship and those conversations. It is designed to help all kindergarten teachers—preservice, novice, and experienced—align their practices with the new expectations and prepare themselves for professional success in the kindergarten classrooms of today and tomorrow.

This book brings together the established developmental kindergarten knowledge base, the current research on standards-based best practices for elementary classrooms, and the most recent findings on human learning. The result is a principled, practical, and effective approach for creating *learning-centered* kindergartens that will help teachers improve their classroom practices and maximize student success. The intent is to integrate major bodies of scholarship that have not been brought together before—the early childhood educational knowledge base that has traditionally informed kindergarten practice and the recent research on standards-based practices in elementary school—in order to create a powerful new foundation for effective practices that reflects both kindergarten's long standing values and commitments and the more contemporary goals that complement federal initiatives. This is a classroom-friendly guide that links research and theory to classroom practice, uses real-world examples to bring ideas to life, and offers concrete, specific strategies that kindergarten teachers will be able to implement in their classrooms immediately.

This book is organized into ten keys. In order to be as user-friendly as possible, the keys are uniformly structured and thoroughly written so that teachers can read them in any order. Each key begins with a brief presentation of the main ideas at the heart of the key, written in a style that is conversational yet rigorous. Important terminology is clarified in a glossary at the end of the book. This is a particularly important feature because each U.S. state uses different language in its standards-based accountability system, and so teachers across the country often use different terms to talk about the same concepts or, even more confusing, the same word about different concepts.

Next, the main ideas are brought to life in a vivid narrative vignette of a successful kindergarten teacher at work. Developed from the author's first hand observations, this "Classroom Snapshot" serves as a case study that presents an exemplar of excellent standards-based practice, portrays effective instructional strategies, and depicts solutions to the complex dilemmas that arise when teaching kindergarten. Practical strategies and tips for implementing the key's main ideas provide additional opportunities for readers to envision incorporating the ideas into their own classroom practices. Tables, photographs, and other visual elements such as templates and forms further help teachers integrate the ideas with their own.

Each key concludes with a discussion that offers clarification and interpretation and provides strong encouragement for kindergarten teachers to embrace these new ideas as a way to become more effective with their students. Engaging with the various perspectives of school practitioners will allow readers to strengthen their connection to the main ideas and to consider the possible implications of adapting the ideas to reflect the specific demands of their school contexts. A concluding checklist summarizing the central points in the chapter helps readers pull the ideas together and offers sound guidance to practitioners aspiring to improve their kindergarten practices. Professional books, carefully selected empirical articles, and other practical materials can all be found in "Helpful Readings to Strengthen Your Knowledge Base"; these resources will further assist kindergarten teachers in developing research-based practices and to grow as professionals

The primary audience for *The Learning-Centered Kindergarten: 10 Keys to Success for Standards-Based Classrooms* is preservice, novice, and veteran kindergarten teachers. Elementary school administrators committed to supporting their kindergarten faculty and mentors working with beginning kindergarten teachers will also benefit from this book. University faculty (both professors and administrators) involved in the preparation of kindergarten teachers should find this book a useful resource as well.

The Learning-Centered Kindergarten: 10 Keys to Success for Standards-Based Classrooms is also an excellent resource for use in:

1. undergraduate preservice teacher education courses focused on kindergarten teaching, guidance of young children in groups, early childhood education, or primary grade education.

2. alternative certification programs preparing prekindergarten, kindergarten, and primary teachers.

3. university postbaccalaureate programs that grant an elementary teaching credential or award a master's degree and elementary credential.

4. university courses preparing graduate assistants to work as student teaching supervisors or facilitators in kindergarten classrooms or practicum courses designed to support student teaching supervisors.

5. graduate courses focused on curriculum and instruction in early childhood education and the primary grades.

6. graduate courses in educational administration focused on instructional leadership or supervision.

7. professional development workshops for mentors working with novice kindergarten teachers.

8. professional development workshops for experienced elementary teachers moving down to kindergarten for the first time.

9. professional development workshops for school librarians, music, art, and physical education teachers who have extensive contact with kindergarten students.

10. staff development workshops for paraprofessionals working in prekindergarten, kindergarten, and primary grade classrooms.

Acknowledgments

I would like to thank all the teachers and colleagues I have worked with over the years, all of whom are a part of this book. Throughout the years, I have been privileged to call some of the finest educators on the planet my friends. We have brainstormed, laughed, and cried together. Our shared experiences are woven throughout this book, and it is with my deepest respect that this book is written.

Finally—a debt of gratitude to my family. To my sister Debbie, who gives the best advice and keeps me out of trouble, and to my mother, who wishes I would follow her advice more. To my loving husband and wonderful sons—you have encouraged, supported, and believed in me. Your patience and sense of humor kept me going. Thank you from the bottom of my heart.

Corwin Press wishes to thank the following peer reviewers for their editorial insight and guidance:

Jenna Bibb
First Grade Teacher
Wilder Waite Elementary School
Dunlap CUSD #323
Peoria, IL

Peggy Campbell-Rush
Author of *I Teach Kindergarten*
Washington, NJ

Christine K. Chaney
Third Grade Teacher
East Side Charter School
Wilmington, DE

Mandy Ellis
Cross Categorical Special Education
    Teacher
Wilder Waite Elementary School
Dunlap CUSD #323
Peoria, IL

Elizabeth Graue
Professor
University of Wisconsin–Madison
Madison, WI

Jill M. Klefstad
Assistant Professor
University of Wisconsin–Stout
Menomonie, WI

Julee A. Loorya
Kindergarten Teacher
Birney Elementary School
Redondo Beach, CA

Betsy Rogers
2003 National Teacher of the Year
School Improvement Specialist
Jefferson County School System
Birmingham, AL

Catherine Schrock
National Board Certified Teacher
Early Childhood Generalist
Classroom Teacher
Detroit Public Schools
Detroit, MI

About the Author

Photo by
Jeanette Peterson

Shari Y. Ehly is an educator with twenty-six years' experience teaching kindergarten, first, and second grade mostly in the Killeen Independent School District (ISD) in Killeen, Texas. After receiving her MEd in Curriculum and Instruction at the University of Texas at Austin, she served as a campus-based instructional specialist, supervised new and veteran teachers, provided professional development for Killeen ISD teachers, and has written curriculum and assessments for the district. She is currently an assistant principal in the same district.

She brings a practitioner's perspective and firsthand observations of real classroom situations and solutions to implementing a learning-centered kindergarten program using a standards-based curriculum. Her experiences as a teacher, campus instructional specialist, and a school administrator give this book the authority to both address the challenges currently facing practitioners as a result of the changing expectations for kindergarten and to expound the practices used by those teachers who have been most effective in adapting to the changes.

Introduction

The Importance of Learning-Centered Kindergarten in Today's Standards-Centered World

When people find out that you teach kindergarten, what kind of response do you receive? Do you get "God bless you! You must be a special person"? Do you hear "Gee, that sounds like a fun job! You must play all day!"? Even professionals in the education profession will often assume that the job you do is less important than that of teachers from "tested" grade levels. After all, there are no real pressures in kindergarten!

If this sounds familiar, you're not alone—all teachers of young children encounter this reaction countless times during their career. Kindergarten often holds a special place in adults' hearts. Their golden memories of kindergarten as a time of simplicity, innocence, and wonder can be powerful and precious. These feelings are made even stronger by the regular appearance of this perfect image of kindergarten in magazine advertisements, movies, and television commercials—is there anything more endearing than a precocious five-year-old? Despite its powerful presence in our memories and in popular culture, in recent years this vision of treasured kindergarten experience has been disappearing rapidly from U.S. public schools

No Child Left Behind, Standards, and Changes in Kindergarten

The No Child Left Behind Act of 2001 (NCLB) requires states to implement accountability systems in which all public school students in grades three through eight are taught challenging standards in reading and mathematics and tested annually to assess their mastery of those standards. Because failure to comply with this law carries significant financial penalties, NCLB prompted most states to develop content standards, adopt standardized testing programs to assess students' mastery of the standards, and require public school districts to align their curricula with the new standards-based accountability systems.

The primary grades and kindergarten were not included in NCLB's call for challenging standards. Nevertheless, the impact of NCLB has been felt strongly at these grade levels. Intense concern about preparing children to enter third grade with the foundational skills necessary to master the third-grade standards and to pass the high-stakes tests has resulted in "accountability shovedown" (Hatch, 2002, p. 457): NCLB's emphasis on student mastery of a predetermined set of learning standards has descended from the upper grades through the primary grades, and all the way down to kindergarten.

NCLB, standards-based education, and accountability shovedown have had a tremendous impact on kindergarten. Beliefs about the specific knowledge and skills that young children should be learning and understandings of the most effective ways to teach that content have been changing rapidly. As a result, today's kindergarten teachers have to contend with many new expectations, new demands, and new obligations.

The Need for Learning-Centered Kindergarten

What can we do to make sure that kindergarten is an environment in which young children's experiences become treasured memories of learning about themselves and the world, making independent choices from an array of exciting activities and interesting materials, connecting with others through play and the arts, and experiencing the thrill of reaching challenging but achievable goals? The answer is simple . . . learning-centered kindergarten! Learning-centered kindergarten teaching is a way to maintain the well-loved practices unique to this wonderful grade level while still satisfying all of the obligations to teach state-mandated standards.

Despite the many changes generated by NCLB, one non-negotiable assumption at the heart of kindergarten has remained constant: Kindergarten is a place where young children learn. Reaffirming the centrality of young children's learning is the first step toward effectively responding to the many new challenges we are facing. Creating a learning-centered kindergarten is a powerful way to combine the traditional purposes of kindergarten—meeting young children's needs across all developmental domains and preparing them for future success in school—and the contemporary purposes of kindergarten—moving young children toward mastery of the academic skills mandated in the state's kindergarten standards—without sacrificing the integrity of either set of purposes.

What Is a Learning-Centered Kindergarten?

According to a recent report from the National Education Association, learning-centered classrooms "are classrooms where teachers focus on student learning and are continuously working to understand new theories about learning and what these mean for their own teaching" (Evertson & Neal, 2006, p. 1). Teaching strategies, curriculum, instructional materials, assessment, classroom management, the organization of the physical environment, and the use of time all share a common focus on supporting student learning and achievement in the learning-centered classroom.

From this perspective learning-centered kindergarten is a classroom in which teachers make the deliberate decision to ensure that *all of their students learn every day.* Learning-centered kindergarten teachers use instructional approaches that allow the mandated content, as well as all other knowledge and skills, to be taught in ways that are meaningful, engaging, and appropriate for all children in their classes. Learning-centered kindergartens honor students' needs, value the process of discovery and meaning-making, and also maintain a focus on purposeful, productive growth toward worthy instructional outcomes.

One can find all of these qualities in learning-centered kindergartens:

- All children learn every day. "All children, no exceptions" is a key feature of learning-centered classrooms. Every child—including those with learning differences, developmental delays, physical challenges, limited English proficiency, accelerated intellectual development, home lives negatively impacted by poverty, and so on—has multiple opportunities each day to experience meaningful, significant learning beyond the standards and to engage with the learning standards at a level and in a manner that is appropriate for them. *All children, no exceptions.*

- Instructional practices are grounded in the most up-to-date understandings of how young children learn.
- Instruction is differentiated in response to the documented needs, strengths, and learning preferences of the students in class.
- Learning means more than just mastering the standards. Five- and six-year-olds must learn and grow in all developmental domains—social, emotional, physical, and cognitive—in order to achieve success in school and in life. In a learning-centered kindergarten, social and emotional learning are an integral part of the curriculum.
- Teachers, like their students, learn every day. Teachers learn while teaching and observing students, through ongoing reflection on teaching, as a result of interactions with students' parents and caregivers, in the context of collaboration with colleagues and administrators, and in other professional development contexts.
- Parents and families are valued partners. Their expansive and multidimensional knowledge about their children contributes in significant ways to kindergarten teachers' ability to be effective with young students.
- Child-centered practices are moved into the twenty-first century. Responding to children's developmental needs and teaching the whole child are not goals of a learning-centered kindergarten. Rather, these become important tools that help kindergarten teachers meet their goal: ensuring that all students learn every day.

Making *Your* Kindergarten a Learning-Centered Classroom

This book offers recommendations to help you put students' learning at the heart of your daily work. Descriptions of learning-centered instructional decision-making are given as well as learning-centered classroom practices, learning-centered perspectives on classroom management, and leaning-centered professional stances. Practical strategies for incorporating these approaches into your teaching are also provided. After reading this book you will know how to

- align your teaching practices with the latest research about how children learn;
- infuse the standards thoroughly into your instruction;
- design lessons that respond to the needs and strengths of all your students and that connect each of them to the standards in meaningful ways; and
- develop tools that clearly show parents, colleagues, and administrators that your practices are rigorous, that your students are learning, and that your curriculum is meeting all district and state expectations.

Having years of experience as a kindergarten teacher, instructional specialist, school administrator, staff developer, researcher, and mom of children with a range of exceptionalities shaped the ideas in this book and guided the efforts to provide you with the keys to success in establishing a learning-centered kindergarten classroom. The goal is to help you experience new levels of professional satisfaction and success as you manage the challenges facing teachers in today's shifting educational climate and to offer strategies that will enable you to meet your students' developmental needs, move them toward mastery of your state's standards, and help them go to first grade knowing that they are competent, capable learners. It's a challenging yet rewarding adventure. Let's get started!

Key 1

Embrace Kindergarten's Multiple Purposes

It is the supreme art of the teacher to awaken joy in creative expression and knowledge.

—Albert Einstein

The Challenges of Teaching Kindergarten Today

The implementation of standards-based accountability systems has had a significant impact on kindergarten and kindergarten teaching. Standards-based education has created an environment where many teachers feel their ability to decide what knowledge and skills to teach their students has been limited. This focus on standards has intensified the implied expectation to cover content and at a breakneck speed. It seems that standards-based education has shifted kindergarten's focus from the learning process, individuality, and developing the whole child to emphasizing learning outcomes, uniformity, academic achievement, and content mastery. But in reality, standards-based accountability systems actually left the most essential responsibilities and decisions at the heart of kindergarten teaching virtually untouched. Every day, kindergarten teachers across the country continue to thoughtfully design learning experiences that enable the specific, individual children in our classes to make meaningful connections with a set of important, valuable ideas and skills. The particular bodies of knowledge being taught may have changed, but the decision making that takes place in order for us to help students forge connections with the curriculum is the same as it ever was.

What does that mean exactly? Just this: Regardless of the standards, kindergarten teachers always have a number of students who struggle with the content and skills presented to them, others who flourish, and still others who are on target. All successful kindergarten teachers take the time and effort necessary to make a personal connection to each student and use the knowledge gained as a tool to move that student forward. The state standards and curriculum may not always be developmentally appropriate for all students in the classroom, but the teacher makes a difference through modifications and adaptations that scaffold the struggling student, support the average student, and accelerate the more advanced student. They do this for *all* of their students, everyday, with no exceptions.

Learning-Centered Kindergarten: A Bridge Between Two Worlds

The image of the teacher as a bridge between the child and the curriculum, first introduced by John Dewey over a century ago, is a powerful metaphor for kindergarten teachers seeking to establish learning-centered kindergartens in standards-based educational environments. Dewey argued that the process of education requires an interaction between the child and the curriculum. He also pointed out that this interaction is mediated, facilitated, and supported by the teacher. In other words, for learning to occur teachers must combine their extensive knowledge of the particular needs, strengths, and interests of the specific students in their classes, their knowledge of the state-mandated kindergarten standards, and their knowledge of effective instructional practices to create experiences custom-designed to connect their students to the standards.

One of the great strengths of this model is that it grants teachers tremendous flexibility and unlimited opportunity for creativity and innovation in the bridge-building process. Rather than squeezing teachers tightly between their obligations to teach the standards and their commitment to meet the developmental needs of the students in their classes, Dewey's perspective allows teachers to be strong, competent professionals who are capable of making informed decisions about teaching and learning.

An essential step in establishing yourself as the bridge between your students and the curriculum is to know the standards fully and deeply. Detailed knowledge of your state's kindergarten standards in all content areas will assist you in identifying all the possible points of connection between your students and the information you are expected to teach, and thereby allow you to maximize your students' opportunities to learn. One way to better familiarize yourself with the standards is to discuss them with your colleagues during grade-level planning. A roundtable discussion that includes not only information about the knowledge, skills, and state expectations but also how your peers address the standards in their classroom can supply you with some very concrete applications.

If you are a novice teacher, please keep in mind that even veteran teachers do not have all the answers or teach in child-friendly and developmentally appropriate ways. Seek out the advice of a professional you trust and respect when looking for a collegial partnership. If collegial conversations do not produce the desired effect, using the standards as a guide while creating learning experiences for your students will keep you focused on what is expected as well as what is needed by your students. In Key Ten there will be a more in-depth discussion about how to accomplish this.

In the next few paragraphs, you will read the first of many Classroom Snapshots. This will illustrate how to apply the strategies from each chapter. The first Classroom Snapshot is about a teacher who manages to pull together the traditional vision for kindergarten and the expectations of the state standards in her learning-centered kindergarten classroom by thoroughly knowing both the state standards and her students.

Classroom Snapshot—Ms. Carlos
Lesson: Sensory Awareness and
Vocabulary Development

Ms. Carlos, a veteran teacher of fifteen years, genuinely enjoys her students and considers them "her kids." This Classroom Snapshot takes place during the second nine weeks of school. Ms. Carlos, as kindergarten teachers do, has laid the groundwork in her classroom by spending the first few weeks of school teaching her students classroom procedures such as behavioral expectations during learning centers, cleaning up work areas, how to participate in small group situations, and what to do if a question arises while Ms. Carlo is working with other students. She is also instilling a belief in her students that learning everyday is *their* responsibility and it is not optional. Because of this final expectation, each child is eager to come to school because they know they will learn *something*.

In the following scenario, Ms. Carlos is presenting a lesson about the five senses. The importance of this particular lesson was made clear to Ms. Carlos after a pretesting activity the previous week and the conversations that ensued. Using a senses game, Ms. Carlos had the students sniff scent jars to distinguish and name the scent. The scents ranged from a variety of fruity scents to soap, flowers, etc. (See the Resources in the back of this book for instructions on how to make your own scent jars.) During the activity, she realized that the many of the students used the term *bubble gum* to associate the natural fruity and minty scents. She knew many of her students were from low economic households. Was it possible they had not experienced tasting and smelling the different fruits in their natural states? She began casually asking her students (usually during snack time) about the types of foods they ate at home, trips to the grocery store, and so forth. She gathered from these casual conversations that many of her students had not experienced fresh fruits and vegetables. While they did have fresh fruit at school and many of them had the canned variety at home, many of the students did not have the developed working vocabulary to name a variety of fresh produce. From these conversations, the lesson below was created. You will see

how Ms. Carlos uses this lesson to address many state standards (listed below in detail) and meet the individual needs of the students at the same time through the learning centers that follow the whole group activity.

State Standards

Science: Scientific Process. The student uses age-appropriate tools and models to verify that organisms and objects and parts of organisms and objects can be observed, described, and measured. The student is expected to identify and use senses as tools of observation; and make observations using tools including hand lenses, balances, cups, bowls, and computers.

Science: Scientific Process. The student develops abilities necessary to do scientific inquiry in the field and the classroom. The student is expected to ask questions about organisms, objects, and events; plan and conduct simple descriptive investigations; gather information using simple equipment and tools to extend the senses; construct reasonable explanations using information; and communicates findings about simple investigations.

Math: Probability and Statistics. The student constructs and uses graphs of real objects or pictures to answer questions. The student is expected to construct graphs using real objects or pictures in order to answer questions and use information from a graph of real objects or pictures in order to answer questions.

Math: Patterns, Relationships, and Algebraic Thinking. The student identifies, extends, and creates patterns. The student is expected to identify, extend, and create patterns of sounds, physical movement, and concrete objects.

Language Arts: Listening/Speaking/Culture. The student listens and speaks to gain knowledge of his or her own culture, the culture of others, and the common elements of cultures. The student is expected to connect experiences and ideas with those of others through speaking and listening.

Language Arts: Listening/Speaking/Purposes. The student listens attentively and engages in a variety of oral language experiences. The student is expected to respond

appropriately and courteously to directions and questions and listen critically to interpret and evaluate.

Language Arts: Listening/Speaking/Communication. The student communicates clearly by putting thoughts and feelings into spoken words. The student is expected to learn the vocabulary of school such as numbers, shapes, colors, directions, and categories; use vocabulary to describe clearly ideas, feelings, and experiences; clarify and support spoken messages using appropriate props such as objects pictures, or charts; and retell a spoken message by summarizing or clarifying.

Language Arts: Reading/Vocabulary Development. The student develops an extensive vocabulary. The student is expected to discuss meanings of words and develop vocabulary through meaningful and concrete experiences; develop vocabulary by listening to and discussing both familiar and conceptually challenging selections read aloud.

Language Arts: Writing/Spelling/Penmanship. The student composes original texts. The student is expected to dictate messages such as news and stories for others to write; write labels, notes, and captions for illustrations, possessions, charts, and centers and write to record ideas and reflections.

Whole Group Activity

The children sit on the carpet, "crisscross, applesauce," and almost all eyes are on the teacher. Ms. Carlos is at the front of the classroom sitting in her oversized rocking chair with a large, colorful bag beside her. The students eagerly wait to find out what is inside. "Who's ready to learn?" she asks. All hands shoot up into the air. Some students lift onto their knees to get a closer look. A boy sitting next to Ms. Carlos tries to peek inside the bag. Ms. Carlos smiles at him. "Nice try, but not quite yet." The boy smiles back. He knows whatever is in the bag will be fun.

"Look at my bag. Using what you know about the world around you, predict what you *think* is in the bag."

Immediately, all hands shoot into the air. Some students are making a sound of excited urgency to be called upon. "Jonathan, tell me what you think is in the bag and why you think so."

"Well, I think it is a video game," Jonathan states confidently. "The bag is big enough to hold it, 'cause I have one and I know how big they are."

"That's a pretty good prediction based on what you know." Other children are called upon and share their predictions. They are as varied as the students themselves—some predictions more possible than others. As the students share their ideas, Ms. Carlos gives them more information as to what could be in the bag.

"Let me give you a clue. All great scientists work from clues and make predictions from their clues. The first clue is this: There is more than one item in the bag. With this new information, what do you think is in the bag?" The students continue to make predictions and Ms. Carlos gives another clue—something you can find on a farm, in a grocery store, and something the Very Hungry Caterpillar would like. Within a short time, a child guesses fruit. Indeed there were a variety of fruits in the bag. Ms. Carlos takes out a blindfold and tells her students that they will be using their senses to help them describe the fruits. She has purposefully chosen some fruits the children are familiar with as well as exotic choices. She calls Anthony, the class "scientist," up to sit beside her. She blindfolds him and explains that he will taste the fruit and describe it using his sense of smell and taste. (Important note: Ms. Carlos previously reviewed health cards to check for allergies.) She pulls an apple out of the bag. She hands Anthony and the other children a piece of the apple. She has instructed the students that they are not to give any hints, but they can experience it with him.

Anthony smells the apple slice but cannot describe the apple. He then tastes it and knows that it is an apple. Ms. Carlos writes the word *apple* on chart paper and draws an apple beside the word.

"How did you know that it was an apple?" she asks.

"It tasted like apple."

"Describe how it tastes and feels in your mouth."

"It is crunchy and good."

Ms. Carlos writes *crunchy* and *good* on the chart paper. "Okay. What else?"

"It is a little bit sweet, but a little bit sour."

Ms. Carlos takes the blindfold off the student and writes the words *sweet* and *sour* on the chart paper. "Anthony, the words sweet and sour are opposites. Can you explain how the apple can be both sweet and sour?"

"It was sweet when I first tasted it, but when I bit it, it was a little bit sour."

"That is excellent work! Who would like to add some descriptive words?" The students share their descriptions and Ms. Carlos adds them to the chart—*wet, juicy, hard*. After a few minutes of sharing, she continues the process through the choices of fruits: pear, papaya, banana, strawberries, oranges, watermelon, and grapes. The students have an opportunity to try each and give a description. Not all fruits are accepted with the same eagerness, but Ms. Carlos encourages the students to try them and compare the tastes and textures "in the name of science."

As the children taste, Ms. Carlos questions them about prior experiences: Have you tasted this before? Where in the world do you think this fruit comes from? What type of plant do you think it grows on? The discussion provides the students an opportunity to share what they know, experience problem solving situations, and share personal information with their peers, thus building a community in the classroom.

After the lesson, Ms. Carlos explains the work the children will be doing in each of the learning centers. She walks from center to center, explaining and reviewing the expectations and procedures from each area. Ms. Carlos uses the learning centers to spiral skills and experiences previously taught to the students in a new and novel way, as well as to provide a time for her to work in small groups or independently with students. The students are called to learning centers today by shirt color. Each child is allowed to choose where he or she will work. They collect a list of centers that they can mark off as they complete each one. (See the Resources in the back of this book for a description of procedures for successful centers and for examples of center checklists.) As in many kindergarten classrooms,

Ms. Carlos uses a thematic approach to teaching her students. Today, fruit is the vehicle by which the teacher continues the theme from her whole group activity to provide varied and novel experiences in all subjects. The following describes how Ms. Carlos modifies each center to meet student needs and abilities.

Learning Centers

1. **Scented play dough.** This center provides students an opportunity to use and develop fine motor muscles while benefiting from other sensory experiences. The students enjoy creating fruit shapes and "cookies" using cookie cutters. (See the Resources at the back of this book for a scented play dough recipe.) Conversations are lively and enthusiastic as language development abounds. The students discuss the fruity scents of the play dough—not just "bubble gum." Success!!

2. **Scented painting.** The students attempt to draw a still life of fruits using scented paint (or scented markers) and color their drawing with the same scent as the fruit. Learners begin by drawing fruit shapes with pencils and then filling in the shapes with paint. Scented watercolor paint consists of unsweetened fruit drink powder mixed with water. Use less water than directed to intensify the color and provide a thicker consistency.

3. **Patterning with fruit**. This math activity revisits a skill using fruit as a novel way to increase interest for students. Ms. Carlos uses a parent volunteer at this center, but if that is not available to you, the teacher could monitor this center to ensure the fruits were managed in an acceptable way and to facilitate conversations. The students are allowed to create fruit kabobs using fruits from the morning activity. Students must create a pattern and duplicate the pattern visually on a recording sheet. The difficulty of the pattern will depend upon the ability of the student. Students are also given a choice in how to represent

the pattern on the recording sheet as well as justifying their choices. Each fruit kabob is placed on a paper plate, marked with the appropriate student's name, and put into a refrigerator to be consumed by the creator during afternoon snack. This center will be replaced on day two with fruit-shaped stamps so students can create patterns without the need for replenishing fruits each day. All students will need to participate in this center on day one if the kabobs are going to be used as afternoon snack, or the teacher must allow the students an opportunity to create one during snack time.

4. **Fruity graphs.** This math activity allows students an opportunity to create a graph using fruit-shaped erasers. Graphing is not a new skill or concept for these children, but the spiraling of this skill provides problem solving experiences in a familiar way. In this activity, each child takes a handful of erasers and draws the corresponding number of each fruit on the graph. This activity can be modified for students with learning challenges by using a buddy system, parent volunteer, or adapting the materials: using fewer choices of fruit shapes; allowing for fewer of each choice; allowing students to use fruit-shaped stamps or stickers instead of drawing on the graph; or finding fruit-shaped clip art for students to cut and paste onto the graph. As students become more proficient at graphing, problem-solving questions can be added to the activity—for example, how many fruits were from trees? How many more fruits had covering that need to be removed than fruits with covering you can eat?

5. **Journal writing.** Journal writing is a learning center activity that is a constant in Ms. Carlos's room. The students must come to this center daily. Using different writing prompts or props to inspire their writing—sometimes using tracers, stickers, or ink pads and rubber stamps to help draw the picture which provokes a writing topic—the learners grow and develop a sense of self through writing. The writing expectations Ms. Carlos has for the students' journal follow the developmental stages of the individual student,

She allows and accepts their writing attempts, while encouraging them to grow and develop. Today's writing prompt is a response to the learning activity in whole group. The students write about something they learned and share their opinions about the different fruits they tasted. They begin by drawing a picture and then write about the experience. When they are ready to move to the next center, they bring their journal to Ms. Carlos and explain what they have written. For students who are in the pre-writing stages, Ms. Carlos takes dictation for them. Some students use the words written on the chart from the lesson to help them write the words they need. (See the Resources in the back of this book for a sample writing prompt.)

6. **Listening center.** The listening center is another constant in Ms. Carlos's room. At least weekly, the students listen and respond to a story on tape. Ms. Carlos gives the students a different purpose for listening each week, which revolves around language development, concepts in print and phonemic awareness, and reading comprehension. This week's selection, *The Very Hungry Caterpillar* by Eric Carle, is a classroom favorite. The students record the sequence of events in the story using pictures and words when possible.

7. **Science exploration**. The children compare attributes and elements of each fruit using their senses and a hand lens. Using a recording sheet to document their findings, the students share their observations about the size, shape, color, smell, textures, and seeds of each item through invented spellings and drawings. Today, Ms. Carlos assists the students by taking dictation of their observations and comments as well as guiding them through thoughtful discussions about the fruit and the use of their senses. She will use these observations as part of an assessment of the whole group activity.

8. **Grocery store**. In the housekeeping area, students use old cardboard boxes, plastic food, plastic jars and food containers, and other items to create a grocery store.

Ms. Carlos leaves plenty of newsprint and markers in the learning center so the students are able to create sales flyers and signs. Ads from the local Sunday newspaper add environmental print and a real-world connection to this learning center; this also facilitates and encourages writing. Baby dolls, dress-up clothing, and a toy shopping cart complete the area for an enjoyable language and cultural experience.

9. **Computers**. The students always enjoy using the computer. Another way standards are met in Ms. Carlos's room, the computer allows students to practice skills, create products such as books or pictures, read stories, or learn through interactive videos to reinforce skills learned in class. Today, Ms. Carlos chose a site (http://www.dole5aday.com) where the students can play educational games or listen to music and watch a video about the benefits of eating five helpings of fruits and vegetables a day.

10. **Sand table.** The sand table is another favorite in the classroom. Today the students compare and explore the capacity of jars and containers. This center is used daily and the information and skills gained from this experience resurface when Ms. Carlos discusses measurement later in the year.

11. **Blocks.** Blocks are another staple in Ms. Carlos's classroom. The blocks are for pure student enjoyment, development of spatial relationships, problem solving, creative and vocabulary development, as well as developing social skills.

Reflection on the Classroom Snapshot

Teaching the standards in a developmentally appropriate way is an obvious solution to the challenge of integrating the standards into our existing kindergarten practices. As illustrated by the Classroom Snapshot, Ms. Carlos utilizes her depth of knowledge about her students—the discussions and discovery of her students' inexperience and lack of knowledge about real fruit—and her knowledge of the standards to create a lesson that is developmentally appropriate for all students while meeting the state expectations. Ms. Carlos frequently reads the state standards when she is creating lessons and discusses them with colleagues during grade-level planning meetings. It is the time and effort spent to understand the state standards and her students that helps her align the lessons to meet her students' needs.

As illustrated in the Classroom Snapshot, thorough knowledge of the standards and a deep understanding of students' abilities allow teachers to take a proactive stance and help others, such as administrators, parents, and colleagues, see the outstanding opportunities for meaningful learning experiences. Newsletters to parents and other public forms of communication that deliberately highlight the specific standards being taught in child-centered, play-based lessons are a way to communicate that the standards are an explicit and visible part of classroom life. A classroom or hallway bulletin board becomes more than a way to share student work; it becomes a billboard that demonstrates the connection between the standards and students' work, especially when they include labels designed to highlight that important information. (This is discussed further in Key 9.)

Beginning kindergarten teachers—whether novices just entering the profession or experienced teachers moving to kindergarten from another grade level—are fortunate to be able to weave the standards into their kindergarten practices from the start. Though they need time and guidance to develop the skills necessary to teach young learners effectively, beginning kindergarten teachers have the opportunity to lead the way in establishing a professional perspective in which deep knowledge of the standards and a strong commitment to meeting the varying needs of their students are understood to be inseparable partners.

Guiding Principles and Practical Strategies

When reflecting upon your teaching and practices in a learning-centered classroom, it is important to shift your professional focus from accountability to responsibility. Accountability may be the official term preferred by administrators and legislators, but this word fails to capture the deep ethical and interpersonal engagement that is fundamental to teaching kindergarten. Rather than being driven by a need for accountability, kindergarten teachers are motivated by a commitment to responsibility to the students in their classes, to the students' parents and families, to the students' futures, and to the democratic goals and purposes of public school. Positioning the need to teach the standards as a professional responsibility rather than a bureaucratic obligation will help us to find a comfortable place for the standards in our caring, learning-centered kindergarten classrooms.

Strategy: Form study groups to look closely at the standards.

Collaborate with kindergarten teachers at your campus or schools in your district to deepen your knowledge of the standards and to focus on the relationship between the standards and your curriculum and practices. Your study group might want to

- figure out how the standards fit into your established kindergarten programs;
- develop innovative ways to enrich existing units by incorporating additional standards;
- find ways in which the expertise and knowledge in your students' families can be utilized to strengthen your standards-based lessons; and
- brainstorm ways to modify and adapt lessons to meet the needs of all students.

Remember that your goal is to move your students toward mastery of the knowledge and skills contained in the standards. For teachers faced with the pressure to cover a great deal of content in a short period of time, following your district's scope and sequence or pacing guide—perhaps even checking off the skills that you taught the students and activities you completed with them—can easily become a daily goal. Do not lose sight of your responsibility to the students and their learning. Truly, your daily goal is to move all of the students in your class toward mastery of the standards in a way and at a pace that provides for meaningful learning for each child. The students' learning is the bottom line of teaching.

Strategy: Utilize assessment tools frequently to maintain a strong understanding of your students' growth and learning.

These tools can range can from casual conversations and teacher observations to performance assessments and rubrics. You should use any method available to gain information about each child's interest and growth. Strengthening your knowledge about your students as learners enhances your connection to them, improves your effectiveness in teaching them, and keeps your professional focus on the best, most satisfying part of kindergarten teaching: developing and sustaining meaningful relationships with young children. When evaluating your students' academic progress, don't stop with the screening tools and standardized assessments selected by your district. Make regular, ongoing use of informal, teacher-developed assessment tools that focus more broadly on students' developing competencies, on their beliefs about themselves as learners, and on their growth in the social, emotional, and physical development domains. Here are just a few suggestions.

- Anecdotal observations—kindergarten teachers are masters of observing and diagnosing the needs and strengths of their students. With the current focus of standardized and state or district testing, teachers sometimes question the value or reliability of this important tool.
- Reflective notes—these differ from anecdotal observations in that the teacher is reflecting upon the lesson and overall impact upon the learning community. This exercise provides the teacher with insights of what teaching practices are effective with his or her students.
- Documented conversations—this assessment practice is where the teacher simply transcribes (or records) the conversations of students in a learning situation. The depth of information gained through these conversations can be very powerful: The teacher learns what the students know, what they are interested in learning, how well they problem solve, and the complexity of language development, just to name a few things.
- Learning photographs and video footage—visual documentation of students who are problem solving and working through learning opportunities. A picture *is* worth a thousand words.
- Work samples with supporting documentation or work portfolios—while samples of student work are very valuable, the additional supporting documentation (teacher notes about what was occurring during the assessment) creates a clearer picture of what the student was thinking and the learning process. Organizing the assessment in a way that provides a way to easily collect the data and relay the information to parents and families is vital.

Use Your Professional Knowledge Base to Guide Your Practice

Your professional knowledge base is your number one tool for helping your students master the knowledge and skills presented in the standards. Using the professional knowledge you have acquired in a responsive, creative way will ensure student success. This includes using activities, strategies, and materials that will allow your students to engage with the standards in meaningful and powerful ways.

Strategy: Raise your expectations for your students' achievement far beyond the limitations of the kindergarten standards.

Read more about accommodations recommended for gifted and talented learners and use those strategies in your class to provide intellectual enrichment for all students. Teacher materials by Johnson, Polette, and Kingore suggest high interest, critical thinking and learning opportunities for students of varying ability levels (see "Helpful Readings to Strengthen Your Knowledge Base" at the end of this book). Providing a rigorous curriculum for all students will not diminish the quality of opportunities and experiences you provide for your gifted students. Having time to work with intellectual peers and having choices in topics and activities will challenge more advanced learners and enhance and individualize their learning experiences.

Opportunity for Professional Growth

The obligation to teach the standards can feel like an overwhelming burden to endure; however, it can provide teachers with a wonderful opportunity for professional growth and renewal. Use the new expectations as a springboard for revitalizing your curriculum, refreshing your practices, developing your professional knowledge base, or learning new content.

Strategy: Think outside of the box.

Teachers can use creative methods to teach the standards. The following are good starting points.

- Develop interdisciplinary connections or thematic units across the content areas. In the Classroom Snapshot, Ms. Carlos used a thematic unit on the five senses to make connections across content areas. Fruit was not the focus of the lesson, but it became a vehicle by which the students were able to discover and develop new skills and concepts. By using a multisensory approach, she provided interest and novelty for knowledge and skills being revisited and offered new learning opportunities not yet experienced by some of her students.

- Integrate the arts into your curriculum. Research shows that the arts enhance and enrich the core curriculum for all students, giving them deeper understanding of the content, better problem solving and critical thinking skills, and a more complex lens through which to view and appreciate the world around them (Deasy, 2002). Yet in many school districts the arts—music, drama, and visual art programs—are being cut. Teachers are being asked to provide adequate coverage of this content as well as the content of core subjects. As states focus upon the core subjects in the upper elementary grades, the academic discourse of shoving more into the curriculum of the early childhood grades leaves teachers feeling that the arts are fluff that should be discarded. Putting the arts back into the curriculum adds elements of interest and creativity into normally mundane and repetitive tasks.

- Find ways to move the kids and the learning outdoors and bring real-world applications to concepts learned in the classroom by forming partnerships with community members. Field-based instruction, frequent theme-based walks in the neighborhood, and parades that celebrate learning can all be a part of learners' academic experience. Field trips do not need to be lengthy or costly to provide optimal learning opportunities—simple trips to the local grocery store, walks in the neighborhood, or even around the school can provide numerous teachable moments on a variety of academic levels.
- Partner with an upper-grade teacher to create mixed-age lessons that allow the older and younger students to construct meaning together in activities designed to draw on your knowledge of child-centered, hands-on practices and the upper-grade teacher's knowledge of more complex levels of the skills and concepts being taught.
- Explore the possibilities of using the technology available at your school campus—or technology you use readily in your personal life—in new and exciting ways in the classroom: a digital camera to create books focusing upon a new concept or a presentation for open-house, a video camera to create a movie written and performed by your students, Web pages, podcasting, or e-mail.

Pulling It All Together

When creating a learning-centered classroom, the teacher

- understands that the implementation of standards-based education has changed certain aspects of kindergarten, but that many key features of learning-centered kindergarten teaching remain the same;
- serves as a bridge connecting the students and the curriculum;
- makes informed decisions about teaching and learning based on thorough knowledge of the standards;
- knows more than just the standards, including how students learn and in-depth knowledge about his or her students;
- develops lessons that teach the standards while also addressing the needs of the whole child; and

- is creative and integrates standards from different content areas in a single lesson or revisits prior knowledge and skills to provide students with practice and reinforcement.

Reflection . . .

- How well do you know your students?
- Do you have daily conversations with them?
- How often do you use the information gained from casual conversations with your students to create lessons that are meaningful and interesting to them?
- How do you modify the lessons and activities so that all students can learn?
- How well do you know your state standards?
- What part do standards play in guiding your instruction and creating engaging work for your students?
- How do you communicate the connection between the practices in your classroom and the state standards to others?
- How does your school's curriculum connect to the standards?

Key 2

Understand How Children Learn

If a child can't learn the way we teach, maybe we should teach the way they learn.

—Ignacio Estrada

Learning Theory and Creating a Learning-Centered Kindergarten

How do children learn? In order to create a learning-centered classroom, the teacher must have some idea how to answer that question. There have been volumes written about how humans learn. Researchers have studied everything from the physical inner workings of the brain to how the environment and outside stimuli affect learning to students' learning styles and preferences. All of these theories provide valuable information teachers should be familiar with in order to better understand how to meet the needs of their students. Research about human development and learning styles is at the core of learning-centered classrooms. The studies by Piaget, Vygotsky, Gesell, as well as Gardner and Goleman, theorize that children exhibit different interests at different stages. Their theories of developmental learning encourage context-based learning in the classroom while discouraging an interventionist approach. This emphasis on allowing each child to learn at his or her own pace in an atmosphere of hands-on learning can help classroom teachers make knowledge-able and well-informed decisions about the practices and experiences to provide for their students. More important than *which* theory a teacher decides to put into practice is whether the information is a part of his or her instructional toolkit used to benefit the children.

A learning-centered classroom hinges upon understanding children and how they learn, including their interests and prior knowledge. Gardner's theory of multiple intelligences is an important tool for teachers who want to provide learning experiences for students. Additional research by experts such as Dunn, Dunn, and Perrin (1994), Goleman (1995), and Sternberg (1996) supports the theory that not all students are motivated the same way and that individual children possess their own learning and thinking styles. By recognizing the interests and strengths of the students, the teacher can fine-tune and adapt the lessons offered. Figures 2.1 and 2.2 will assist you as you create engaging student work and better design meaningful activities that meet your students' interests and learning styles.

Student learning can be influenced by a number of other factors: environmental interruptions (announcements, noise level, scheduling), time of day, situations at home (a deployed parent, a seriously ill family member, financial concerns, disruptions in family routine), and basic needs not being met (not getting enough sleep, not having enough food, lack of emotional stability, feeling unsafe). Although a teacher may not have control over many of these influences, being aware of these problems and adjusting expectations to accommodate the student will reassure the child that the school environment is a caring and safe place—one in which they can relax, enjoy, and learn.

Using figures 2.1 and 2.2, you will be able to identify the strategies used by the teacher in the Classroom Snapshot while creating lessons and learning activities for her students. Contained in the next few pages is the snapshot of Ms. Cook's classroom, which illustrates how she uses her pedagogical knowledge to facilitate a yearlong learning experience for her class and their families based on the students' individual learning styles and interests. Ms. Cook is a teacher with five years' experience. She teaches kindergarten in a military community. Travel is a fact of life for military dependents, which provides Ms. Cook with both an excellent learning opportunity for her students and an opportunity to build her classroom community.

Figure 2.1 Gardner's Multiple Intelligences and Activities

Intelligence	Characteristics	Activities of Interest	Prime Learning Opportunities
Verbal/Linguistic	Usually strong vocabulary, enjoys wordplay and all aspects of language—rhyming, talking, reading, listening, writing	Reading, writing, speaking, listening, wordplay	Journaling, mnemonic triggers, labeling, listening centers, word games, memory games
Logical/Mathematical	Enjoys using numbers and problem solving—recognizes patterns	Working with numbers and patterns	Creating patterns, problem solving and critical thinking opportunities, working with numbers
Visual/Spatial	Able to represent ideas artistically, taking things apart, building models, hands-on projects	Working with images, visualizing, drawing, science projects	Using manipulatives, projects, drawing, using clay, painting, assembling puzzles
Musical/Rhythmic	Remembers songs and lyrics quickly, enjoys moving to music and creating it	Using components of music—rhythms, melody, patterned sound, dance movements	Create songs/poems to memorize information, dance and physical movements linked to concepts, add a tune or jingle to activity
Bodily/Kinesthetic	Able to use bodily movements to make connections to solving problems and share ideas	Using sense of touch to interpret and process information—body movements, dramatics	Using sign language, dance, role/dramatic play, using manipulatives, physical games, constructing models
Interpersonal	Works well with others; responsive to moods, feelings, and behaviors of others	Sharing, cooperating, interviewing	Working in cooperative groups, role-playing, Think-Pair-Share, buddy groups, drama/improv activities
Intrapersonal	Thinks in terms of themselves—personal opinions and emotions most important	Works better alone, self-paced, demands personal space	Working independently, self-talk strategies, journaling, living choices for ownership
Naturalist	Deep understanding about the natural world around them	Outdoors person, classifies, sorts, patterns	Labeling it, constructing models, classify objects, find patterns, hands-on experiments, working outdoors and with items from outdoors

SOURCE: Adapted with permission from *Brain-Friendly Strategies for the Inclusion Classroom* (p 51–56), by July Willis. © Alexandria, VA: ASCD. © 2007 by ASCD. Used with permission. Learn more about ASCD at www.ascd.org.

Figure 2.2   Dunn and Dunn Learning Styles and Activities

Learning Style	Characteristics	Activities of Interest	Prime Learning Opportunities
Auditory Learners	Remember best when learned auditorily, but need a variety of formats—can multi-task, may seem to have traits of attention-deficit/hyperactivity disorder (ADHD)	Storytelling or narrative to present information, group participation, activities that incorporate music, Pair-Share, peer tutoring	Cooperative centers, interactive games, wordplay, songs to reinforce concepts
Visual Learners	Need visual cues to make connections to concepts.	Looking at pictures, drawing, watching body language and facial expressions, solving puzzles	Visuals such as graphics, videos, photographs, graphic organizers to organize ideas and share concepts; draw pictures and mind maps to organize thoughts; role-play or use drama to add visual cues to concept
Tactile Learners	Need concrete learning experiences that involve opportunities to handle materials	Using manipulatives and hands-on activities to introduce and reinforce concepts	Touch, smell, taste everything—including others; opportunities for multisensory activities as well as discovery learning; direct teaching limited to small increments of time; bring in music, movement, finger plays, and art
Kinesthetic Learners	Need to move their bodies to make connections, very sensitive to the constraints of the classroom environment, may appear hyperactive or immature for age	Physical body movements, responds well to physical contact with teacher (pats on the back for reassurance), usually good at athletic games—good coordination and motor control	Many of the strategies for tactile learners, physical/athletic games, role-playing, dramatic interpretations, improvisation, mime activities

SOURCE: Adapted with permission from *Brain-Friendly Strategies for the Inclusion Classroom* (p 51–56), by July Willis. © Alexandria, VA: ASCD. © 2007 by ASCD. Used with permission. Learn more about ASCD at www.ascd.org.

Like many teachers, Ms. Cook had heard of the Flat Stanley project. It is an opportunity for learning information about cultures, geography, and social issues of the world through the travels of an imaginary friend (http://www.flatstanley.com/). She took the Flat Stanley project one step further by providing each student with a box and a set of instructions for the parents. The parents were instructed to send Flat Stanley to friends or family members around the world. Flat Stanley was to be returned to the classroom in the box with souvenirs, pictures, news clips, and so forth with a letter from the loved ones explaining Flat Stanley's travel experience. The families were to review the materials and information in the box together so the child could share the contents during class. (See the Resources in the back of this book for a sample letter to families about this Flat Stanley project.)

The following snapshot begins with "Where in the World is Flat Stanley?" time—a weekly, modified show-and-tell event for students to share the items returned in the boxes. Depending upon the items in the box and the interest level of the children, Ms. Cook designed lessons to cover the standards and provide challenging, thought-provoking experiences for her students.

Classroom Snapshot—Ms. Cook
Lesson: Flat Stanley Revisited

State Standards

(For whole group activity only—many standards are met throughout the year as a result of the original lesson.)

Language Arts: Listening/Speaking/Purposes. The student listens attentively and engages actively in a variety of oral language experiences. The student is expected to determine the purpose for listening such as to get information, to solve problems, and to enjoy and appreciate; to respond appropriately and courteously to directions and questions; and to listen critically to interpret and evaluate.

Language Arts: Listening/Speaking/Culture. The student listens and speaks to gain knowledge of his or her own culture, the culture of others, and the common elements of culture. The student is expected to connect experiences and ideas with those of others through speaking and listening, and compare language and oral traditions (family stories) that reflect customs, regions, and cultures.

Language Arts: Listening/Speaking/Audiences/Oral Grammar. The student speaks appropriately to different audiences for different purposes and occasions. The student is expected to ask and answer relevant questions and

make contributions in small or large group discussions; gain increasing control of grammar when speaking such as using subject-verb agreement, complete sentences, and correct tense.

Language Arts: Listening/Speaking/Communication. The student communicates clearly by putting thoughts and feelings into spoken words. The student is expected to use vocabulary to clearly describe ideas, feelings, and experiences; clarify and support spoken messages using appropriate props such as objects, pictures or charts; and retell a spoken message by summarizing or clarifying.

Language Arts: Reading/Vocabulary Development. The student develops an extensive vocabulary. The student is expected to discuss meanings of words and develop vocabulary through meaningful and concrete experiences; develop vocabulary by listening to and discussing both familiar and conceptually challenging selections read aloud; and identify words that name persons, places, or things, and words that name actions.

Social Studies: Geography. The student understands the physical and human characteristics of the environment. The student is expected to identify the physical characteristics of places such as landforms, bodies of water, natural resources, and weather; and identify the human characteristics of places such as types of houses and ways of earning a living.

Social Studies: Culture. The student understands similarities and differences among people. The student is expected to identify personal attributes common to all people such as physical characteristics and identify differences among people.

Social Studies: Culture. The student understands how people learn about themselves through family customs and traditions. The student is expected to identify family customs and traditions and explain their importance; compare family customs and traditions; and describe customs of the local community.

Social Studies Skills. The student communicates in oral and visual forms. The student is expected to express ideas

orally based on knowledge and experiences; and create and interpret visuals including pictures and maps.

Social Studies Skills. The student uses problem solving and decision making skills, working independently and with others in a variety of settings. The student is expected to use a problem solving process to identify a problem, gather information, list and consider options, consider advantages and disadvantages, choose and implement a solution, and evaluate the effectiveness of the solution.

Whole Group Activity

"Everybody have a seat, have a seat, have a seat," sings Ms. Cook to the tune of "Mamma's Little Baby."

"Everybody have a seat on the floor. Everybody have a seat, have a seat, have a seat. Everybody have a seat on the floor. Not on the ceiling, not on the door. Everybody have a seat on the floor." The students hurry to finish cleaning up their areas, put their work into their cubbies, and find their spot on the carpet. Ms. Cook has three boxes on the floor next to her. "Today, we have three Flat Stanley travel treasure boxes to share. Flat Stanley went to visit Kim's grandmother who lives in Seoul, Korea, James's daddy who is stationed in Hamburg, Germany, and Shanna's cousin who lives in San Antonio, Texas. Let's take a look at the globe to see how far he traveled." Ms. Cook has a child retrieve the globe from the shelf, and she shows the students each location and marks each with a different colored sticker so they can get a closer look later during learning centers. Kim, James, and Shannon each have had an opportunity to review and study the items in their boxes during the week, with help from family members at home. The students bring in the boxes when they feel ready to share with the group. For items such as letters or books that need to be read aloud, Ms. Cook steps in for the student as needed.

Before she introduces the student presenters, Ms. Cook reminds the other students about their responsibilities as an audience member. "I want you to remember how to be a good audience member. Eyes on the person who is speaking and your ears are listening to what they

tell you. Remember that you are going to have an opportunity to ask questions. You will also be able to give suggestions as to what we are going to do with the information we learn today—how we are going to learn more about the interesting places and the items in the box."

One by one, the students come to the front of the group and share the contents of their travel treasure boxes. Kim, whose grandmother lives in Seoul, has a wide array of interesting goodies to share with her peers. One of the treats is freshly fried yakimando, a fried Korean eggroll filled with meat and veggies, made by Kim's mother. Ms. Cook had heated them before this learning session so each child could taste them as Kim spoke about the other items. Some of the children do not like the vegetables in the eggrolls, but Ms. Cook reminds them that they do not have to eat it if they do not want to. She also reminds them that they can be polite when passing up the opportunity to try something new. Most of the students decide to try the new tasting opportunity, making the connection between the eggrolls served at school for lunch and the ingredients stuffed inside this eggroll. Conversations about the different shapes of the eggrolls and comparisons of flavors follow.

After the students have an opportunity to taste the yakimando, Ms. Cook plays a videotape of Korean dancers in ceremonial dress and shows them a Korean doll in similar clothing. The children watch as the graceful dancers move about the stage. Ms. Cook asks the students to listen to the different instruments in the music and try to pick out ones they can identify. When the video ends, Kim shares pictures of scenery from the area where her grandmother lives and quite expertly informs the children that the most popular mode of travel in Korea is bus or bike, not cars like here in the United States. She also tells her friends that Seoul is a city like here in the States and the people who live there dress just as they do—jeans, tennis shoes, T-shirts, dresses, pants. The traditional hanbok worn on the doll and the dancers in the video is for special occasions and celebrations.

James and Shanna also have an opportunity to share the contents of their boxes. James's dad, stationed in

Germany, gathered a few items for the class: a recipe for bretzeln (German soft pretzels), a map of Germany, a collection of German coins, and pictures of the area where he is stationed. The students ooh and ahh as they see the snow-covered mountains as well as the magical and beautiful castles. When Shanna shares her box of travel treasures, many of the children comment that they too have been to San Antonio. They make a connection to the pictures of the Alamo, River Walk, Six Flags, and Sea World and want to share their experiences there. Ms. Cook plays the CD of mariachi music for the students as Shanna continues sharing the contents of her box. The students move to the music.

Ms. Cook compliments all of the student presenters and the audience as they have sat for a long time on the carpet area. As promised, she pulls out a chart tablet and markers and allows the students to comment on what they found interesting and ask the three presenters questions about their items. After a few minutes, Ms. Cook creates a chart about the items and asks the students to share what they would like to learn more about—whether it is more about a place or a single item from the boxes. Many of the students want to make the recipe for the soft pretzels; after all, they would be able to taste the finished product. Ms. Cook teases the students, telling them that she would be like the Little Red Hen—she would make the pretzels and then eat them all herself. The entire class excitedly protests that idea and promises they will help her make the pretzels.

Ms. Cook writes all the suggestions on the chart tablet. The students are jumping out of their spaces, eager to share ideas about how they can extend their learning. They do have fabulous ideas! Some of the more intriguing and creative suggestions include creating a scrapbook of the Flat Stanley journeys so everyone could remember and know about the different adventures, locate the places on the globe, look at all the different kinds of money from around the world, create a Journeys learning center table so everyone could get a closer look at the items from the box, and find, cook, and taste other foods from the places where Flat Stanley has been.

One child, Joey, mentions that he is going to be moving in a couple of weeks and is very unhappy that he will not be able to share his treasure box or be able to participate in the fun. Qiana adds that there were others who had moved or will be moving during the year and suggests that the class write to them and ask them to return a Flat Stanley. The other students comment that creating a Flat Stanley would make them feel like they were still a part of their class if they were the ones who had moved away. They also thought it would be a good idea to make a completed scrapbook of all the Flat Stanley journeys for the friends that had moved.

Using What You Know About Your Students

Ms. Cook uses the list compiled by the students, as well as the information she knows about her students through interest inventories, to plan activities during the year. She adds to the list by inviting community members to come and share information about the items and places the students have explored. A proprietor of a local German restaurant comes to share about her native country and brings supplies from her restaurant for a cooking lesson with the children to make the pretzels they had heard about during James's presentation. A travel agent comes and brings brochures of places from around the world and shares a video about some of these interesting places. Parents come and share other items and tell stories about their adventures on journeys they have taken. The art and music teachers participate by sharing fine arts activities focused upon the different cultures and nationalities investigated during their special class times. A word wall is created, and the students learn words from different countries and how they translate to English.

Throughout the year, the students create pages for their travel scrapbooks. They journal, draw pictures, and add items from their boxes. Ms. Cook scans the items from the boxes so the children can all have artifacts from around the world. She makes an extra copy for herself and duplicates it for the students who move. As the year progresses, students who know they are leaving make sure the parents give Ms. Cook their new address; they want to be sure to get the remaining pages from the treasured books and to feel connected to their classroom community.

Reflection on the Classroom Snapshot

The Classroom Snapshot reveals how Ms. Cook combines pedagogical knowledge with knowledge of her students' individual learning styles to create a learning-centered classroom. She modifies and utilizes the Flat Stanley project throughout the year to meet both the expectations of the state standards and the unique needs of her students. As part of her daily routine, though not specifically illustrated in the snapshot, Ms. Cook gains information from her students through the use of graphing. This leads to a strategy for successful teaching in her learning-centered classroom.

Strategy: Learn about your students' interests and learning styles through reinforced and revisited skills in activities such as graphing or the use of glyphs.

Each day Ms. Cook writes a statement on chart paper that is posted near the door. The statement solicits the student's personal opinion or participation in a particular activity, such as "My favorite flavor of ice cream is . . ." or "On the weekend I enjoy . . ." When students enter Ms. Cook's classroom, they place a self-stick note with a smiley face or the child's name in the column or line of their response choice to represent their personal answer. By responding to important questions or finishing a statement, they reveal their interests and learning styles. Here are some other examples Ms. Cook might use.

I learn best when:
  I work alone
  I work with others
I like working with numbers
  Yes   No
I remember best when:
  I hear it and talk about it   I sing it   I move with it
  I draw something   I feel it   I see it

Through the use of the graphs and glyphs, teachers can gain information and use it as a springboard for conversations in the classroom, thus building a supportive and safe community. This valuable data about the students' learning styles and interests can also be used when creating learning opportunities that provide reinforcement and enrichment of skills needed by students to solve problems.

In the Classroom Snapshot, Ms. Cook allowed students to provide ideas and input for future learning activities. Even though all activities brainstormed may not have appealed to all students' learning styles, they were valued by all because the ideas were generated within their peer learning community. The fact that Ms. Cook respected them as learners affirmed that she cared about them and thus provided a safe and meaningful learning environment for them. The ideas inspired by the students were varied and provided multisensory experiences for all. Ms. Cook enhanced these learning opportunities by involving members of the local community, as well as parents, and asking them to share their expertise and experiences with her students.

Strategy: Allow students the opportunity to gain ownership in the learning activities.

As illustrated by the Classroom Snapshot, a simple conversation with the students can produce wonderful ideas for learning opportunities that will be valued and meaningful to the learners. Problem solving is a skill that is developed through practice and modeling. Some students may have difficulty with providing input at first. However, after they gain some experience through repeated opportunities to share and interact with the ideas of peers, and they are more comfortable with themselves as learners, the ideas will come more readily and will be more creative.

Possibly the most impressive activity suggested by the students was the idea to continue the connection with the students who had moved away. It shows the value of each member of the classroom community and the significance of their ideas instilled and reinforced by the teacher. Some military students put up emotional barriers because of the pain felt when parents and friends are deployed or moved to other areas. Even at the tender age of five, these students realized the importance of feeling a part of the community and keeping in touch with those who go far away. Thank goodness Ms. Cook understood this need in her class and provided an outlet for this emotional issue.

This leads to another very vital piece of the learning-centered classroom and the next strategy.

Strategy: Provide a safe learning community.

This strategy could take up a book all by itself, but it would begin with the teacher gaining the trust of the students and their families. Trust is complicated, and the ways to obtain that trust are as diverse as the students in your classroom. One way to gain trust is to show that you care about your students and respect them in all ways—culturally, emotionally, socially, and intellectually.

Ms. Cook gains the trust of her students and their families through the conversations she has with them. In the Classroom Snapshot, she demonstrates how she values the students' ideas by creating learning opportunities for them borne from their ideas and by adapting those ideas to their optimal learning style. She regularly speaks to the parents to keep abreast of issues and is sensitive to the needs of the families as she accommodates and adapts for these situations. This is not as difficult as it sounds. Adaptations can be as easy as providing reading material for the student who doesn't have books at home or being sensitive to single parent families with multiple jobs. These parents may want to help their children, but are just not at home, able to assist, or have the funds for materials needed to complete projects. Ensuring the child receives the extra help and support at school—with permission or agreement from the parent—provides the child and the family with a safe learning community and trust in you as the teacher.

Pulling It All Together

When creating a learning-centered classroom, the teacher

- uses his or her pedagogical knowledge about how students learn with the knowledge gained about the students to create meaningful learning experiences;
- adapts the learning experiences to meet the needs of the students;
- provides students with an opportunity to take ownership in the learning experiences; and
- involves the community and families in the learning experiences.

Reflection . . .

- How well do I know all of my students and their learning styles?
- What activities do I provide to gain information from my students?
- Do I know enough about how students learn and learning styles?
- What can I do to involve the community and families in the learning process?
- Do I use the learning styles models when creating lessons for my students?
- How could this improve the learning experiences for my students?
- Do all of my students feel the classroom is a safe learning environment?
- Do I create learning opportunities with all students in mind or do I shoot for the middle?

Key 3

Recognize the Special Needs Child

*All of us do not have equal talent, but all of us should have an
equal opportunity to develop those talents.*

—John F. Kennedy

Identifying Special Needs Students in Kindergarten

Because the purpose of a learning-centered classroom is to ensure all
students learn every day, no exceptions, then a teacher must be able to
identify and address the requirements of a special needs student.
Because kindergarten is the first formal educational experience some
children encounter, many kindergarten students with learning disabilities or other conditions have not yet been diagnosed or identified, and
rightfully so. No one wants to prematurely "label" a child. After all,
who's to say a child just isn't developmentally ready for a particular
skill or concept? Perhaps the child hasn't had the necessary educational
opportunities prior to coming to school to help him or her succeed.
Maybe the child has experienced a traumatic or upsetting situation at

Material used throughout the chapter from the National Autism Association
(http://www.nationalautismassociation.org) is used with permission. Material also
reprinted with permission from the *Diagnostic and Statistical Manual of Mental
Disorders*, Fourth Edition, Text Revision, © 2000. American Psychiatric Association.

home that interfered with the learning process. Or possibly the family has moved frequently and there have been gaps in learning concepts.

In his book, *A Mind at a Time,* Mel Levine describes how everyone learns differently. In the adult world these differences are often valued and accepted, especially when the individual is a creative thinker. Levine points out how children are often misdiagnosed, mislabeled, and overmedicated in an effort to make them behave and learn in the same way as their peers. He suggests that teachers not only nurture the strengths of each child, but try to figure out which teaching strategies will best scaffold and support the learning weaknesses of the student. These strategies include learning about the interests of the student in order to motive and engage him or her, as well as knowing what pre-learning skills are needed to accomplish deep understanding of each concept.

Kindergarten teachers must know what is within the accepted range of development in order to determine if students are progressing appropriately. Without this information, it is impossible to effectively assess students and create appropriate work for them. Although a trained health care provider will make the actual diagnosis of cognitive and developmental challenges, knowing what to do for children with learning differences will prove a valuable teaching tool for you. The following chart (Figure 3.1) lists characteristics of most five-year-olds without developmental delays. This chart can assist you in determining if a child could be developmentally delayed in a variety of academic areas. It is also a good tool to use when communicating with the child's parents.

Teachers must remember that every child, even those with similar learning challenges, is different. Parents know how to motivate and encourage their child through difficult tasks. While the environment at school is very different from home, the cues and strategies that work at home can often be modified for school use. The information presented in this chapter has been modified to give teachers a better understanding of the general needs of students. It is in no way a substitute for seeking information about individual students from parents and professionals familiar with that student.

In the Classroom Snapshot, Ms. Washington has numerous students with varying learning challenges. She finds that by providing a learning-centered classroom she not only maximizes their learning, but also enriches the learning of all students.

Figure 3.1   Benchmarks and Developmental Expectations
for Five-Year-Olds

Gross Motor	Fine Motor	Pre-Reading	Writing	Mathematical Concepts	Social/ Emotional
Hops on one foot	Completes puzzles with 10 pieces	Knows personal information—birthday, address, and phone number	Traces letters and shapes	Understands ordinal numbers	Organizes and cares for personal items
Bounces and catches a ball	Can pick up objects using pincer grip	Distinguishes between upper-case and lower-case letters	Correctly writes name	Counts objects to 20	Solves problems independently
Walks forward and backward in a straight line	Strings beads in a pattern	Correctly sequences four pictures	Knowledge of print aware-ness—top, bottom, left, right, front, back of book	Comprehends concept of addition and subtraction	Accepts and adjusts to changes in routine and transitions
Gallops, skips, and jumps	Ties shoes, buttons and zips own clothing	Responds to open-ended questions	Draws simple shapes and colors beyond scribbling	Identifies coins	Works and plays cooperatively with others
Alternates feet going down stairs	Can control scissors and paste pictures on paper	Demonstrates story sense—beginning, middle, end, characters, plot, setting	Draws a person with at least six body parts	Understands relationships—big/little; in/out; over/under; thick/thin; more/less	Shows concern for others
Stands on one foot for 10 seconds	Builds with blocks	Recites nursery rhymes	Dictates a story	Identifies shapes and attributes	Recognizes authority
Throws a ball	Carries own plate of food	Repeats a six-to-eight word sentence	Uses new vocabulary in conversation and writing	Problem solves real-world situations using mathematical concepts	Accepts routine chores and responsibilities
Marches	Can perform finger plays	Retells a story	Identifies differences between letters and numbers	Masters one-to-one corre-spondence	Meets visitors without shyness
Runs	Can create 3-D shapes from clay	Answers questions about a short story	Controls crayons and pencils easily and with proper grip	Can graph objects by attributes	Cares for per-sonal needs—going to the restroom, brushing teeth, dressing self

SOURCE: American Academy of Pediatrics, http://www.aap.org/healthtopics/stages.cfm.

Identification and Modification

Identifying the academic needs of students is a difficult task at best. Teachers are not pediatricians; yet an experienced teacher can identify commonalities in struggling students and recommend strategies and teaching practices that can support them. In 2004, Congress reauthorized the Individuals with Disabilities Education Act (IDEA) to focus resources on supporting students who are struggling in school. The act now requires early interventions for students in kindergarten through grade three. The law states that highly qualified teachers will use scientifically based instructional practices to address the behavioral and academic needs of all children. The process is called Response to Intervention (RtI) and usually involves a multitiered approach to assessing struggling students and collaborating with parents, colleagues, and other professionals to find appropriate teaching strategies. In the next section, a few of the learning challenges students face are addressed along with some suggested strategies for dealing with them.

Behavioral and Academic Challenges

Attention-Deficit/Hyperactivity Disorder (ADHD)

First—know your students' strengths and weaknesses. Just as with any student, knowing the unique interests, strengths, and weaknesses of a student with ADHD will provide you with information about when, why, and how inattentive, hyper, or impulsive the child can be. Then you can choose appropriate modifications and teaching strategies to meet the needs of that child. If the child is diagnosed with ADHD and qualifies for special education services, the special education teacher will create an individualized educational program (IEP) to ensure these strategies are integrated with the educational opportunities provided to all students in the class.

Students with ADHD are more successful when clear guidelines and structural procedures are in place in the classroom. They may be able to sustain focus better if they receive frequent reinforcement or work in small groups. The following strategies and practices are beneficial for enhancing the learning opportunities for all students, regardless of their ability (additional strategies will be discussed later in this chapter).

Academic Instruction

The most effective instructional strategy for teaching students with ADHD is to begin with a carefully structured lesson. This means clearly explaining what the child is expected to learn, reminding him or her of prior knowledge that is linked to this learning opportunity, and illustrating how this will benefit him or her personally. When introducing the lesson, you should help the student get organized by visually modeling what is expected in both procedure and product. You should set clear learning and behavioral expectations so that there are no questions about how to proceed. Specify what materials will be needed and where to find these materials if they are not in an area where the student is working. It is best to have the materials at hand, ready for use. Provide the student with a backup plan if he or she cannot remember what to do or follow the directions. Assign the student a peer buddy who can help with instructions, or give the student a picture map or graphic of the steps and procedures to follow. Breaking the instructions down into simpler terms, providing choices, and creating a timetable for completing tasks will provide the student with the support needed to be successful.

During direct instruction, you should provide structure and consistency in the scheduling and format of the lessons. Transitions are difficult for many young children and more so for students with ADHD. Preparing the student for transitional times (such as announcing that the class will be moving from one activity to another in five minutes) can mean the difference between keeping the child on task and having an emotional meltdown in the classroom. Teachers should perform ongoing student evaluations (with all children) to watch for signs of daydreaming or frustration. Implementing the buddy system during learning center time can help keep children with ADHD on task.

Some students may benefit from individual follow-up directions. After the whole class has been given directions for an activity, the teacher can quietly ask the student with ADHD to repeat the steps and directions to ensure he or she understands what to do. If the student has difficulty following multiple-step directions, the teacher should break them down into smaller tasks, so the student can feel a sense of completion and success throughout the process.

Playing quiet music in the background helps some students because it keeps the noise level down. Although conversation during activities is often a wonderful part of the learning process, it also can be very distracting for some students. Again, knowing the children in your room and their learning styles will guide you to making the best decisions for your class.

Here are more strategies that benefit students with ADHD and other learning disabilities.

- Use cooperative learning groups.
- Make the instruction and activities more visual by using assistive technology, such as computers and overhead projectors.
- Help instill impulse control by providing special cues to indicate that students will be called upon next.
- Remind students to keep focused upon the assigned task.
- Allow flexibility for moving around the room, as long as it does not distract or interfere in the learning of others. If the child cannot remain seated and prefers to stand or lie on the floor to complete assignments, provide a space for the child to do so.
- Provide a squeeze ball or bit of clay for the child to manipulate during direct instruction to give an outlet for excess energy during "focus" times.
- Allow students to use headphones to drown out excess noise, if necessary.

Reprinted with permission from the *Diagnostic and Statistical Manual of Mental Disorders*, Fourth Edition, Text Revision, © 2000. American Psychiatric Association.

Autism Spectrum Disorders

Students diagnosed with autism spectrum disorders (ASD), which are part of a broader category of disorders called pervasive developmental disorders (PDD), can exhibit a wide range of social/emotional, intellectual, and developmental delays from an early age. Children with ASD do not follow the same patterns of development as most childrens. Parents usually are the first to recognize that there is a problem; however the National Institute of Mental Health states that "only 50 percent of children are diagnosed before kindergarten" (http://www.nimh.nih.gov). Because of this, teachers may find the following information and strategies (including those found on the charts at the end of this chapter) helpful when working with students who share these characteristics.

Social Interaction

When adults think of children, they imagine social beings, eager to interact with others, craving attention and acceptance. Children with ASD may resist making eye contact with others or interacting with peers or adults—they may avoid cuddling, hugging, and seeking comfort. Some children may lack the ability to interpret facial expressions, making it difficult for them to understand others and connect at an emotional level. Parents of a child with ASD may feel frustrated as they may not have experienced the typical behaviors expected in a parent-child relationship. The simple pleasure of even playing with their child may have not occurred, as these children often prefer playing and working alone. This tendency may lead to intentional misbehavior in the classroom as a way to escape social situations.

Children with ASD may not understand how their actions affect others, and they may not grasp the subtle cues during daily classroom interactions. Without the ability to interpret facial expressions or body language, these children may feel confused or frustrated. This frustration and confusion can often surface in emotional outbursts. They may break objects, attack others, or try to injure themselves.

Communication Skills

Children with ASD may face communication challenges ranging from muteness to developmental delays to only slight language difficulties. For those who are able to develop language, many use unnatural rhythms, pitch, or speech patterns. For example, a child with ASD may speak with a singsong or robot-like voice. He or she may have difficulty holding a conversation or making complete sentences. Since a child with ASD has difficulty relating to others emotionally, the conversation may be very one-sided—with the child droning on and on about their favorite topic, unaware that others may want to participate.

A lack of communication skills often leads to undesired behavioral outbursts. Unable to express what they need or want, children with ASD may scream, grab, or become out of control. The inability of these children to interpret body language and facial expressions makes managing outbursts equally frustrating for caring adults.

Patterns of Behavior, Interests, and Activities

Children with ASD may exhibit unexpected behaviors with an unusual preoccupation with one or more patterns of interest, such as watching a particular object or performing repetitive body movements (e.g., hand rubbing, arm flapping, spinning or pacing around the room). The preoccupation may manifest around certain people or at certain times, which is why routines and schedules are very important for children with ASD. Teachers can provide these students with a picture chart of upcoming events for the day, allowing the student to physically move the picture from the sequence to a pocket as the events occur or as they are about to transition into another activity or situation. A picture book with the people the child will be interacting with in each situation could also be beneficial.

Now that some of the many challenges have been revealed, what is a kindergarten teacher to do? How can one person possibly provide the learning opportunities necessary for these special needs children? Here are some suggested activities from the National Autism Association (http://www.nationalautismassociation.org).

Music therapy is the use of music and its elements (such as sound, rhythm, melody, and harmony) by a qualified music therapist. It can be used with an individual or in a group setting and is designed to promote communication skills to meet the social, emotional, and cognitive needs of the child. Although the classroom teacher is most likely not a qualified therapist, being aware of the effects music may have on the students is important.

According to Prelude Music Therapy (as cited at http://www.nationalautismassociation.org), the top ten therapeutic characteristics of music are as follows.

1. It stimulates and encompasses many parts of the brain to help maintain attention.

2. It can easily be adapted to reflect the child's abilities.

3. It provides an enjoyable context for repetition.

4. It structures time in an easily understandable way—when the song is over, we are finished.

5. It can provide a safe and structured setting for communicating—both verbally and nonverbally.

6. It creates an effective memory aid.

7. It supports and encourages movement.

8. It taps into emotions.

9. It provides immediate feedback in nonverbal ways.

10. Everyone can participate successfully.

Physical or Occupational Therapy

Children with ASD may benefit from physical or occupational therapy if they have any of the following indicators:

- increased muscle stiffness or tightness;

- delay in reaching motor milestones;
- poor balance and poor coordination;
- difficulty in moving through the learning environment;
- postural abnormalities;
- muscle weakness; and
- pain.

The physical therapist or the parent may instruct the teacher regarding ways to help the student with these physical discomforts and disabilities.

Speech Therapy

Since ASD affects speech, the student may need speech therapy to facilitate language. If the child has been identified as autistic and qualifies for special education services, the teacher should inquire if speech therapy is a part of the IEP. If so, the school's speech therapist should be able to provide some practical strategies for classroom use.

In addition to the professional treatments and resources already discussed, some practical classroom strategies (which can benefit all students) are listed below.

- Use art activities—painting, sculpting with clay, drawing, and creating collages—to build fine motor skills and provide a way to express feelings.
- Allow students to use picture cue cards to communicate.
- Provide a picture schedule of activities and persons associated with these activities.
- Give a five- and a two-minute warning before a transition takes place. Use a visual timer to show beginning and ending time.
- Create songs and use music to commit concepts to memory. This provides an energy outlet while promoting listening discrimination, as well as helping to wean children from visual cues. This also helps ease into transitional times and promote positive behavior.
- Allow students to have an easy or desired activity before and after a difficult one.
- Give children choices (e.g., flexible seating, choice of writing utensils, order of work to be accomplished) to help them gain a sense of control.
- Pair certain rewards and positive reinforcers with work activities only—do not use these in conjunction with other activities.
- Provide frequent, short breaks between work sessions.
- Allow children to take a sensory break if necessary.

- Create a reward plan for completion of work and a separate plan for rewarding good behavior. For instance, if students enjoy computer time, they may earn fifteen minutes of computer time for a day without screaming or yelling. Reward plans should include visual charts to track behaviors and rewards.
- Give each child a special place in line that is consistently his or hers, such as third in line, since many kindergarten teachers assign line leaders and cabooses as "helpers." This will allow each child to know where to go when it is time to line up.

Strategy: Don't forget about safety!

Many times children with ASD will hurt themselves or others, or try to escape by running. As a teacher, you need to be aware of the signs of agitation and frustration, so you can de-escalate the situation and head off any episodes before they happen. If an incident occurs, you must have a plan in place to ensure the safety of all children. You may need to solicit the help of your administrators, other classroom teachers, instructional assistants, and other faculty members. Consider these scenarios—what would you do if a child

- ran out of the classroom, building, and/or down the street?
- turned over furniture or other school equipment?
- wouldn't stop screaming?

Although these are just a few of the situations that could happen, it is better to be prepared than to frantically try to put something in place in the heat of the moment. Here are some suggestions: use child protection devices on doors to prevent the student from running out unescorted; provide appropriate training for school personnel who will be working with the student; and learn as much as you can about the student from the parent.

Lack of Educational Opportunities

A study by Hart and Risley (1995) revealed that the economic status of a family impacts the success or failure of a child in school more strongly than race or gender. The frequency of varied vocabulary in conversation, lack of positive messages, and educational opportunities provided by families with different economic standings were dramatically different and predetermined the child's ability to function in an early childhood classroom. Although a child's economic status is not a final, decisive factor for academic success, an effective teacher will be aware of the possible need for intervention. Many children of economically challenged families do not have the same "lap experiences"—those experiences of a child sitting on a parent's lap, listening to stories, talking about the pictures and participating in word play—as children of middle- and upper-class families.

Students who enter school with a delayed working vocabulary often will struggle with school their entire academic career. Studies indicate that this is compounded by a small window of opportunity—ages three to six—to develop that portion of the brain (Healy, 1990). Knowing this, kindergarten teachers must make building that vocabulary for all children one of their primary missions for the year. By providing a diverse vocabulary and print rich environment for their students, teachers open a world of new possibilities for them.

Teachers who support learning-centered classrooms know the importance of language and vocabulary development for all students and realize that the cognitive development of a child can be in concert with the child's social/emotional development. The following practical strategies can increase vocabulary and cognitive development and can be adapted to match skill levels of all students.

- Provide a language rich environment.
- Label objects and actions.
- Provide explanations and rationales.
- Read to students numerous times daily with discussions of text read.
- Give students the opportunity for conversations during circle time and other groupings.
- Model use of rich vocabulary.
- Use open-ended questions.
- Require clarification and justification of answers.
- Build vocabulary through reading the daily news.
- Create word walls—highlighting words and meanings and patterns in language.
- Utilize listening centers—providing more auditory connections to language.
- Use poetry and songs to develop language usage and wordplay.
- Play word games.

Strategy: Experience first.

It is well known that field trips and discovery learning experiences are effective tools for enriching learning. Many times teachers will provide lengthy units devoted to zoo animals or community helpers and then get the kids on the bus to see what they have learned in real life. What is proposed here is that the real learning experience—the field trip or discovery learning experience—is given to the students first, before the lesson. This gives the children a real-world connection before the lesson is taught, provides vocabulary, and stimulates rich conversations with students. All of these things help students to link learning and cement the concepts in their minds.

The Gifted Child

Two common misconceptions surround gifted children: They will learn no matter what is placed before them, and a gifted child is gifted in everything. In many classrooms, gifted children are not provided as challenging a curriculum as their normally developing peers or, if they are gifted in one area, they are only challenged in areas of weakness. In a learning-centered classroom, all children are challenged and learn every day, no exceptions. Some modifications for an intellectually advanced learner could include:

- opportunities to make choices about challenging activities;
- projects and service learning; and
- opportunities to meet and work with intellectual peers—even students in upper grades if there is not a gifted and talented program.

Classroom Snapshot—Ms. Washington

Ms. Washington is a teacher with six years' experience. Because of her ability to quickly identify student strengths and challenges and modify the curriculum accordingly for the maximum progress of her students, her principal places special-needs students in her classroom. This year Ms. Washington is assigned several students with varied challenges, including Lennon, a bright child with cerebral palsy; Mark, a hard-of-hearing student; and Chelsea, a visually impaired student. There are also three students who have not been diagnosed with ADHD, but whose parents are concerned about their inability to focus and displays of inappropriate impulsivity. Each of these parents requested that their child be placed in a classroom with a teacher who "is patient" with active children.

Ms. Washington is not formally trained in special education but seems to have a special understanding for meeting these needs. She has access to an aide two half days a week to assist her. She also has a good working relationship with the children's parents and quickly recruits parents through her monthly newsletter to volunteer in her classroom. She also communicates with parents through daily personal "happy notes" and phone calls to students' homes.

At the beginning of the year, when Ms. Washington discovers that one-third of her class has significant learning needs, she questions whether she will be able to meet the challenge. She is concerned about the other students in her class and wonders if her special-needs children will demand so much of her time that it will diminish her effectiveness as a teacher for her other students. She also is concerned about the safety of the students with physical impairments—how will she be able to do her routine learning activities, such as frequent walks in the neighborhood, multisensory activities, and field trips, with students who are limited in ability and, at the same time, ensure their safety?

These concerns motivate her to research the conditions and appropriate modifications for each child's special need through conversations with the child's parents, special education teachers, and support staff at her school. She also carefully reviews the IEPs for all of the special-needs students to ensure she is meeting the modifications necessary for accomplishing their goals. Through collaboration with the parents and professionals, she gains information necessary to prepare for the students and to make adaptations for them. She also finds that her concerns, while valid, are soon put to rest.

A Little About the Class

Mark is an active and intelligent five-year-old who was equipped with a hearing aid as a toddler. He knows and uses sign language as well as tries to communicate orally. To facilitate this, the teacher wears a personal FM transmitter—a special device with a transmitter and a micro-

phone that sends the teacher's voice into the student's hearing aid.

Chelsea is an intelligent and extremely animated albino African-American child, who is legally blind. She is able to see movement, colors, and magnified objects on a page. She wears thick glasses when she remembers to bring them to school.

Lennon is physically challenged with cerebral palsy. His physical disability mildly affects his speech, but his motor skills are more severely affected. Diagnosed with mixed cerebral palsy, he has uncontrolled movement of his upper body muscles (especially in his arms) and restricted movement of fine motor muscles (such as his fingers). He does not use a wheel chair. He is extremely bright and is motivated to be just like the other students, demanding to be allowed to do things on his own.

Jason, Jonathan, and Tiffany are three very active students who lack impulse control and the ability focus for more than a few minutes. They all seem to have above-average vocabulary skills, but Jonathan has difficulty recognizing his name and identifying certain letters.

Having done her homework prior to the beginning of school, Ms. Washington makes the following modifications to the classroom to accommodate her special-needs students.

Room Arrangement

Movement about the room is always a priority in Ms. Washington's classroom, but with the special needs students in her classroom it becomes even more of a focus. Mark, Chelsea, Lennon, Jason, Jonathan, and Tiffany need the seating arrangements to be flexible for different reasons. Mark and Chelsea need the best vantage point to gain maximum information. Jason, Jonathan, and Tiffany need to be able to MOVE! By allowing them the flexibility to move closer (or to the back of the room in order to not distract other students) she provides them an opportunity to get the wiggles out and still attend to directions and instruction they need to be successful. Lennon also needs plenty of space to move about, so Ms. Washington places the carpet in the middle of the room with tables around

the perimeter to provide him easy access to any table or learning area with the added space he needs. This also provides additional space for movement when the whole group meets on the carpet.

Instructional Strategies

In addition to changing the physical arrangement of the furniture, Ms. Washington makes simple changes to the way she instructs the class in order to accommodate her students. For instance, she does not stand in front of the windows when speaking to the class to ensure that Mark can see her face. Using a natural speaking voice paired with a signing interpreter, Ms. Washington uses varied vocabulary, continually gives definitions and synonyms, and rephrases comments from the other students so that Mark can hear them. She provides many more visuals— bright charts, posters, large photographs and manipulatives—to reinforce the concepts taught to better assist Chelsea and Mark. The use of enlarged print becomes a very necessary tool in assisting Chelsea and allowing her to successfully complete the same activities as her peers. She provides more multisensory activities to ensure that in every lesson all students are able to feel, smell, and taste to add another connection to new concepts. As a result, all the students benefit. The use of multisensory activities and learning sign language provides all students with a richer and more fulfilling learning experience.

Ms. Washington modifies the activities to meet the learning needs of her students. It soon becomes apparent to her that having students with physical challenges isn't as stressful as she had imagined. She does need to plan ahead to make some minor modifications, but this is a standard procedure for all students. Each center and learning activity is multileveled to accommodate the different learning levels of the students. It is a very natural process for her to make the changes necessary to accommodate the physical needs of Chelsea, Mark, and Lennon.

Originally, Ms. Washington thought she would need to modify her favorite part of the curriculum—the field trips and neighborhood walks. This is not the case. She plans

extended time for the walks and provides an adult escort for the physically challenged students. The other students are paired with a classmate. During the walks, Ms. Washington stops frequently, gathers the students around and allows them to use their senses. She then asks them to describe in vivid detail the visual, textural, and fragrant elements of the world around them. Once back in the classroom, with collected treasures, the students create journals to reinforce the new and rich vocabulary from their excursion.

The use of cooperative learning groups and pair-share buddies proves to be even more beneficial as a modification for her special needs students. Jason, Jonathan, and Tiffany benefit by having someone paired with them to keep them focused; Mark, Chelsea, and Lennon are able to work in groups and have assistance when necessary. All the children enjoy working together, and the motivation exhibited by the three physically impaired students encourages their classmates to try harder.

Reflection on the Classroom Snapshot

Through simple modifications and some thorough planning, Ms. Washington is able to provide enriching, meaningful, and appropriate learning experiences for all her students. The students with special learning needs were a gift, as they became valued friends and helped inspire the other students to overcome whatever challenges they might encounter. Soon they were not considered "students with special needs" any more than the rest of the students, as all children have unique learning needs.

Pulling It All Together

When creating a learning-centered classroom, the teacher

- identifies and understands the needs of each student;
- uses school personnel, parental input, and research to find appropriate strategies and modifications for students;
- makes modifications to procedures, classroom arrangement, and activities to support student success; and
- maintains contact with parents to monitor changes of medication, therapy, or other physical conditions.

Reflection . . .

- What do I know about the needs of my students?
- Do I have the knowledge necessary to effectively serve the needs of my students with learning and physical disabilities?
- Do I know and follow the IEPs for my special needs students?
- What modifications do I make for my students?
- How can I better serve the needs of all students to ensure everyone learns, every day, no exceptions?

Key 4

Develop Behavioral Expectations and Procedures

If civilization is to survive, we must cultivate the science of human relationships—the ability of all peoples, of all kinds, to live together in the same world at peace.

—Franklin Delano Roosevelt

Creating a Learning Environment

This chapter is one of the most important of the book and the most difficult. It is a challenge to advise new teachers about behavioral expectations and procedures because their students are as varied as the strategies to handle them. If a teacher is to be successful in creating a learning-centered environment—one where every child learns, every day, no exceptions—there must be a sense of order, respect, and trust in the classroom community. Without these components, even the most engaging and interesting learning opportunities can quickly become a chaotic free-for-all, where no one learns.

Creating a safe and inviting environment comes with providing clear, consistent, and attainable expectations for all members of the classroom community. This is done by:

1. knowing what behaviors are acceptable in your classroom and school or district;

2. modeling and sharing with your students what is expected;

3. providing praise for appropriate behaviors; and

4. applying consistent and appropriate correction of inappropriate behaviors.

It is advisable for teachers new to kindergarten (or to the teaching profession) to sit down with more experienced teachers to discuss which procedures work best for such things as learning centers, what to do with completed work, how students get materials, going to the restroom, what to do during transitional moments, behaviors expected during whole group instruction, and how to handle emergencies such as fire drills.

Consider learning center procedures. It is very important to take time early in the year to instill the expectations for what is acceptable behavior. This takes several weeks, but the time invested results in a pleasant working and learning environment for the students and teacher alike. The teacher shares the behavioral expectations. Perhaps students need to know what to do if the teacher is working with a group and a student in another group has a question. Disruptions can be remedied by having an ask-three-before-asking-me rule: the student asks three friends at the table about the activity or materials before interrupting the teacher. The teacher should have clearly marked baskets or assigned areas for students to put completed work. There should be clear directions posted at each learning center, and the teacher should provide ample instructional time prior to turning the children loose to do independent work. We will investigate these procedures more deeply during the Classroom Snapshot later in this chapter. Keep in mind that the individual teacher is ultimately the final judge as to what will work in the classroom, what the teacher can tolerate in the way of behaviors, and what the students are capable of performing. The procedures you select should reflect those expectations. It also goes without saying that the procedures and expectations should be age-appropriate for the students—expectations that are too difficult will result in escalated misbehavior.

Once the teacher knows what the expectations will be, he or she should communicate them with the students frequently. Students need to be reminded about the rules and procedures, and understand that they have not changed. Being specific about classroom procedures and having the students role-play them the first few weeks of school helps to provide a good foundation for a smoothly functioning classroom. The teacher will need to constantly monitor and reinforce positive compliance of the procedures. Obviously, you do not include rules or consequences you are unwilling to enforce, or enforce anything in a way that would embarrass or devalue the student. This negates your efforts to build trust in your learning community and can cause more serious behavioral issues later.

When procedures and expectations are in place, the behaviors one should expect to see in a learning-centered classroom are movement, conversation, and a variety of learning areas with flexible seating arrangements that encourage students to work alone or in groups. Part of the success in this scenario stems from a well-planned room arrangement. While room arrangement does not guarantee compliance of the rules, rooms that are poorly planned can contribute to problems.

Rooms that are cluttered or have areas that are obstructed from view are conducive to off-task behaviors. The teacher should be able to see all students at all times. Tents, enclosed reading areas, sectioned off areas and cubbyholes provide students not only with a quiet space but also an opportunity for unsupervised behavior. Traffic areas and access to frequently used materials should be accessible. In addition, the room should look inviting and cheerful. The teacher should use professional judgment as to what that means, based upon the personalities and learning styles of the students.

Photo by Linda Wood

Photo by Linda Wood

Does this mean that by following these guidelines there will never be any discipline problems? Not at all. Even in the best of classrooms there are behavioral issues. However, a determining factor as to how serious the issue becomes is the manner in which the teacher addresses the problem. Does he or she de-escalate the situation by quickly identifying a problem and reacting sensitively when a student becomes agitated? Or does he or she escalate the situation, becoming entangled in a power struggle with the student? Are the other children aware of students with chronic behavioral issues, and do they know what to do when there is a problem, such as ignoring inappropriate behaviors or reporting the problem to the teacher?

Most off-task behaviors are minor: students talking during instruction, not completing work or following directions, and minor squabbles with classmates. These are easily remedied, usually with a gentle reminder or a conversation with the student. Behavior charts (see Resources at the back of this book) to monitor progress and success can help students become more productive and cooperative members of the learning community. For behaviors of a more chronic nature, the teacher can manage them by consistently applying some of the following strategies.

- Redirect, or remind students of expected behavior. This can be in a general way: "One, two, three—all eyes on me." If the off-task behavior continues, in a more direct way, "Janice, please look at me while I am teaching. You will need to know how to do this when you go to centers."
- Constantly monitor students so off-task behaviors do not get out of control.
- Monitor student ability level and appropriateness of assignments. Academic expectations that are too difficult or too easy can contribute to undesirable behavior.
- Move to a closer proximity to the disruptive child—make eye contact.
- Use nonverbal cues to stop misbehaviors.
- Keep parents informed of positive and negative behaviors in the classroom and work together to find a successful solution.
- In the instance of serious behavioral issues including fighting, inappropriate language, and tantrums, the teacher must take action as directed by school policy—again, keeping parents informed of situations.

Consequences and Rewards

Student behavioral issues are less likely to occur if the student takes ownership of his or her behavior. Students with chronic behavioral issues should be included when creating a behavior success plan. The student, parent, and teacher should decide what consequences and rewards will be used in order to maximize desired behaviors. Consequences are not punishments and should not create negative emotions from the student. They should be able to make the connection between the behavior and the consequence. The consequence should be logical and fit the behavior. Frequent use of consequences is less effective than prevalent positive reinforcement of successful accomplishments. It cannot be stressed enough—a key aspect to effective classroom management is consistency.

It is also important to note that rewards are not bribes. Rewards such as extra computer or free time, choices of centers, stickers on completed work or behavior charts, and verbal praise from authority figures (such as an administrator) can increase intrinsic motivation for learning and complying with behavioral expectations. It is the goal of positive reinforcement that the student will prefer the positive attention and gravitate towards the desired behaviors.

Common Causes of Misbehavior

When a child misbehaves in a classroom, it is not without reason. When a child is off-task, valuable learning time is lost. As with all learning experiences, the teacher must discover what causes the misconduct in order to provide appropriate modifications to the structure of the environment to ensure success. Some children misbehave as an escape from unpleasant or difficult tasks. Other behavioral issues stem from a variety of underlying causes which can include physical or mental limitations (see Key 3). Through observation and conversations with the student, the student's parents, and the school counselor, the teacher can identify what is causing the problem and together everyone can create a plan for success. What follows are some examples of common behavioral issues in the classroom and some suggested strategies for dealing with each of them.

Attention-Getting

Many children with attention-deficit/hyperactivity disorder (ADHD), and sometimes others, seek the attention of peers and authority figures. Even though many times the attention they receive is negative, this does not persuade them to change behaviors. Allowing these students to be helpers, planning special one-on-one time with the teacher, and giving them a choice of special privileges for compliance with the rules is often successful. Keep in mind that children with ADHD are not necessarily in control of their behaviors, and a plan needs to be worked out with parents and the student to help the student develop self-control and a positive self-image.

Most students gain attention through more acceptable channels. For some students, however, misbehaving is the only way they know will consistently gain attention. Some common ways these students seek attention is by shouting out answers and comments without permission or making strange noises which force class or teacher attention. While this may generate undesired feelings of annoyance and agitation for the teacher, it is best to realize the source and address it in a professional manner.

Aggression

There are many reasons why a child might display aggressive behavior as well as for the intensity of the behaviors themselves. Tantrums, hitting, kicking, biting, and throwing objects are just a few behaviors that can occur. The reasons behind these behaviors are varied and need to be investigated by the teacher. Some important questions to ask during this investigation include: Is the material or activity too difficult for the student? Does the student have sufficient communication skills, or is he or she feeling frustrated, scared, or angry and unable to share those feelings? Are there family issues? Have you observed signs of abuse or neglect? Is there a learning or behavioral disorder causing these outbursts? Does this behavior also occur at home? Consult with the school counselor and get a professional opinion about what can be done to remedy these behaviors.

If aggressive behaviors become routine, create a plan of action for removing the other students quickly in order to ensure their safety and to remove the audience for the misbehaving child. If the child is angry and out of control, the teacher needs to remain composed, speaking quietly and firmly for the student to calm down. Do not expect an out-of-control child to be reasonable. His or her brain is not allowing a calm response and the child will not be able to hear or comply with your request until he or she is returned to a state of composure.

Distraction Due to Basic Needs Not Being Met

The child who fidgets, frequently cries, daydreams, falls asleep, feels anxious or angry, comes to school irritable, or has a pattern of misbehavior around ten o'clock may be experiencing deprivation of basic needs such as food, sleep, and safety. Many times, the young child doesn't have the ability to verbalize or perhaps even cognitively know what is wrong. Do not assume just because a student is not participating in the free or reduced lunch program that he or she has had enough to eat. There are many families who are too proud to accept help. In more affluent families, the child may have not taken the time to eat breakfast. Many children just do not eat properly and are malnourished for a variety of reasons.

Feeding a hungry child is the easiest fix at school. Although most schools have a breakfast and lunch program (and may even provide a snack during the day), some children just do not have enough to eat. The teacher may notice that the child hoards food to take home or quickly eats and requests seconds. If the student comes in late, he or she may not have had an opportunity to eat breakfast. Keeping an additional snack on hand and a place for the child to eat it is an accommodation most teachers can make.

Some children do not get enough rest because of traumatic or unstable situations at home, personal worries, or illness. These children often have difficulty in complying with rules and procedures, following directions, and completing schoolwork. These home situations can also leave children feeling anxious and afraid. Building a trusting relationship with the family is very important here, as well as being sensitive to the child's need to rest. Depriving these children of recess and opportunities to socialize in order to complete assignments could be counterproductive and create more serious behavioral issues. Being supportive to the family and the student usually results in better behavior.

Escapism

When escapism is the motivation for off-task behavior, the student will not complete work, is distractible and distracts others, may react angrily, and will do just about anything to keep from doing what he or she is told. These children are trying to protect themselves by escaping possible adverse consequences from failure. Such misconduct will decrease in a safe learning environment where students are free from ridicule, where ideas are welcome and respected, where cooperative learning groups support students, and where activities are appropriate to the learners' abilities.

Examine this motivation of misbehavior closely. Escaping from emotional pain is a powerful motivator, and people will go to great lengths to avoid such pain—in some situations even committing suicide. Although this is not common in kindergarten, the teacher nonetheless must be sensitive to this need and ensure all students are and feel successful.

Power Struggles

Students exhibiting misbehaviors with power as their motivation will express it by defiant or disrespectful outbursts and refusals to follow the rules. These students feel defeated if they do as they are told and will do whatever is necessary to save face in front of their peers. Teachers who feel threatened when this is the cause of misbehavior can escalate the situation by forcing the issue. Telling the child what is expected and walking away, allowing him or her the opportunity to make the choice to comply is a strategy that works. In addition, providing the student with opportunities to be in leadership positions, as long as he or she is able to handle it, can give the student an outlet as well as a chance to display appropriate behavior.

Self-Esteem Issues

Some students may have difficulty completing tasks and following directions because they expect to fail. They may act out or create reasons for not being able to comply with teacher directives. Teachers recognize that these students are not meeting their potential and sometimes think they are just unmotivated or lazy. Teachers can help these students change their self-image by showing sensitivity, offering encouragement, and providing work that is appropriate to ensure success.

Classroom Snapshot—Ms. Hunter

In the following Classroom Snapshot, Ms. Hunter illustrates the importance of having procedures in place in order to provide a learning-centered classroom. She is a teacher with fifteen years' experience teaching kindergarten at an inner-city elementary school.

The snapshot begins during the first two weeks of school. Ms. Hunter has been focusing on building the learning community and training her students in the acceptable procedures and rules for the classroom. She knows that without these in place, learning opportunities will be lost.

This snapshot highlights a whole group activity where the teacher reviews and practices the procedures for math centers. She has been informally assessing the students since the first day of school to get a better idea of their abilities and has organized the students in similar-ability cooperative groups for learning centers. She has a picture chart at the front of the room illustrating each of the centers the students will rotate to for the day. A laminated picture of each child is attached to the chart with a magnet. Each child locates his or her picture to find out where to begin the learning center rotation. The children remain in their groups throughout the rotation, which consists of five learning centers, twenty minutes per center. These are flexible groups that change over time with activities and student ability.

Beginning-of-the-Year Procedures

The children are gathered on the carpet. Ms. Hunter plays a counting game with the students using linking cubes, plastic bowls, and numeral cards. In this game, Ms. Hunter shows the children a numeral from zero to ten and says the name of the numeral. Then the students build a train with the cubes. When Ms. Hunter says "break it up," the students break up the train into the bowl. Ms. Hunter then asks how many cubes are in the bowl, and the students figure out the number. She plays this game with the children for several minutes, allowing each child a turn at responding to questions and being the "announcer," or the person who chooses the number. This is a game that she will put into learning centers later in the week, so she wants to ensure that the students understand what to do in both roles.

The students are already doing a great job of following directions and using the materials appropriately. Ms. Hunter has clearly explained her expectations for using the math tools during groups, learning centers, and large group situations. When the students are given the linking cubes, Ms. Hunter gives them a few minutes to "play"—they may build a tower, make a pattern, whatever they would like— just to get the initial excitement worked out. Then, on her cue, the cubes turn into math tools designed to help them learn about numbers and math concepts. Ms. Hunter has strict guidelines for using the materials. The students do not touch them until she gives them the "go" sign. They may not throw the cubes or chew on them.

Each time she introduces a new math material, Ms. Hunter has the students role-play different scenarios about "what would happen if . . ." so the children can visualize the causes and effects of common issues. The students then problem solve and verbally share why some behaviors are inappropriate. The consequence for not using the materials appropriately is loss of privilege to use the materials for that session. This seems to be pretty effective, as no one has pushed the issue.

When the game is finished, Ms. Hunter moves from table to table, modeling what each child will do. Later in

the year she will group them by ability, but at this time of year most students are more or less at the same level. The activities at the centers all utilize exploring materials, pattern blocks, linking cubes, teddy bear counters, and attribute blocks. At every math center the necessary math materials, assorted markers, crayons, and blank paper are placed in a basket in the middle of each table. These items have been introduced along with guidelines for using them, putting them away, and how to rotate from center to center.

At the fifth table there is a present—the new math material to be introduced today. Just as in the previous four days, Ms. Hunter shakes the present and asks the children to predict what is in the box. She calls on a student who looks ready to learn to come to the front of the group to open the box. Today's surprise math manipulative is color tiles. Ms. Hunter asks the students to describe the item and discuss possible uses and role-play safety procedures.

Soon the students are ready to be called to centers. Their goal is to freely explore the math tools and create whatever they choose. When Ms. Hunter rings the bell, the students are given a few minutes to record what they created in a drawing. The students then pair up with a partner to share what they drew and discuss briefly what they learned. During this time, Ms. Hunter is walking around, monitoring, and taking notes. At her signal—two dings on the bell—the students put the materials into the basket, collect their recording sheets, and proceed to the table to their right.

Correcting Behaviors

During the second round of centers, a squabble breaks out between two girls over the community crayon basket. The two girls are yelling and grabbing crayons from each other. Ms. Hunter goes to the table to investigate. Before she can make it to the table, crayons are broken and one of the girls is crying.

Tiffany: Sarah took my crayons and won't give them back! Then she broke them!

Sarah: That's not right! She wasn't using them; she just took all the colors and wouldn't share them. She grabbed them and broke some.

Tiffany: I was using them! I get all the colors I need at one time.

Ms. Hunter: So, let's look at the colors. The basket is full of crayons. Are there more of these in the basket?

Sarah: Not that blue one, and it's my favorite. Now it is broken.

Ms. Hunter: So how can we fix this problem?

Tiffany: We can take the paper off and still use it. Then we can each get part of it.

Ms. Hunter: Does that sound like a good plan to you, Sarah?

Sarah [nodding]: I guess. It's not as good, but it will still work.

Ms. Hunter: What can we do next time to keep this from happening again?

Tiffany: Talk to each other and ask to share.

Sarah: Yeah, share.

Ms. Hunter: That sounds like a good plan. Thank you for working this out. Are you ready to get back to work?

Both girls nod. Tiffany takes the broken pieces, removes the paper and hands Sarah a piece of her favorite color.

Making the Connection to Learning

After the children have had an opportunity to go to all five centers, Ms. Hunter calls them back to the carpet. She has the students use their recording sheets to remind them what they learned at each center, and she records their comments on chart paper. Students are given the opportunity to share what they learned and compare or ask questions about the activities. Ms. Hunter uses this as both a review and an opportunity to make a connection from the centers to desired learning concepts. She also uses this time to help reinforce the appropriate vocabulary. Finally, she uses this information as an informal assessment of her students.

Reflection on the Classroom Snapshot

Ms. Hunter's use of clear expectations facilitates and enriches the engaging work she has provided for her students. The students know what she wants them to do and what is acceptable. Although there will always be situations like the crayon incident that will arise, most of them will be minor. If the girls had escalated the situation—for instance if Tiffany had struck Sarah—Ms. Hunter would have needed to go into a more direct mode of discipline management. She would have needed to make sure Sarah was not hurt, and then calmly talked the girls through the process as she did in the example but with a consequence for Tiffany. Consequences for not following the rules are set up at the beginning of the year; they are reviewed daily for the first week, and then the student repeats the rule as violations occur.

If a student strikes others on a regular basis, the teacher, child, parent, and possibly an administrator or counselor should meet to create a plan of action for correcting the problem as soon as possible. Children hit others for a variety of different reasons—none of which are acceptable. Methods for handling the situation vary depending upon the motivation and the child. Kindergarten teachers and administrators are limited in what can be done. The consequences appropriate for older children, such as in-school suspension, are not appropriate for young children. Teachers must follow the guidelines and procedures deemed appropriate by their campus and district.

The most important thing to remember is all children should come to school feeling safe. If one child regularly hits or intimidates others, everyone's learning is impacted in a negative way. The situation should be corrected as soon as possible so all children can learn at maximum levels every day.

There will be problems. It is important to remember that even the best teachers—no matter what they do to match the learning with the child or how close a relationship they have with the child—experience times when a child will misbehave or need to have an office referral. This does not make for a bad teacher or a bad child; it is just a part of life and growing. When a child has behavioral issues and situations at home that the teacher cannot control, all the teacher can do is be as supportive and caring as possible and make appropriate modifications to help correct the problem. It is during these times that the teacher needs to speak to his or her mentor, campus counselor, and campus administrator to request assistance and guidance. They will be a good resource for ideas for handling such situations.

Pulling It All Together

When creating a learning-centered classroom, the teacher

- invests time to teaching the students proper classroom procedures;
- allows the students opportunities to predict and problem-solve scenarios and role-play situations that could arise; and
- provides ample time for the students to use the materials and to link the use of the materials with learning.

Reflection . . .

- How can I improve the procedures in my classroom?
- What causes the most difficulty in my classroom?
- What are the campus or district procedures for discipline?
- Do I have clear procedures in place?
- Am I consistent with the rules and procedures I have set in my classroom?

Key 5

Create a Supportive and Engaging Learning Environment

The real process of education should be the process of learning to think through the application of real problems.

—John Dewey

Classroom Design

The goal of every teacher is to create a supportive and engaging learning environment. The best way to do that, however, is not the same in every classroom. There are many variables that influence the learning environment, ranging from the demographics of the students to the establishment of procedures and expectations to curriculum and instructional practices to arrangement of the furnishings. Some of these topics were addressed in Key 4, and although this chapter will briefly address behavior management, the focus will be upon the teacher's responsibility for making decisions that *prevent* inappropriate student behavior and thus maximize learning. When creating a supportive and engaging learning environment, the teacher of a learning-centered kindergarten must consider the whole child, providing a foundation for success in all aspects of the child's life through meaningful learning experiences that stimulate a desire to learn and develop a positive self-image. It is a huge and important job. No wonder kindergarten teachers feel as if the weight of the world is on their shoulders!

Teachers know that long before the students cross the threshold of the classroom, there is much planning, organizing, and strategizing. If you are a beginning teacher, this may be the first time you have ever put a classroom together. If so, take a seat, look around your classroom, and take a deep breath—the work is about to begin. The first step is to think about the physical environment of the classroom.

Classroom design and the effect of room arrangement on student learning has been widely studied (Good & Brophy, 2000; Wong & Wong, 1993). Researchers have concluded that the organization of the physical environment can deeply impact the depth of learning a child acquires. The Reggio Emilia approach (Edwards, Gandini, & Forman, 1998) goes so far as to consider the environment to be another teacher, one that has the power to facilitate learning. This can happen through a variety of ways including identifying and eliminating possible distractions; moving items or individuals to minimize distractions; providing maximum access to instructional areas and materials and learning areas; ensuring that materials, equipment, and furniture are age appropriate; and providing opportunities for the outside environment to be experienced inside. Some of these suggestions were mentioned briefly in Key 3 in reference to the needs of students with physical challenges, but the use of space and materials should be considered for all students. Here are some things to consider.

- The room should have clearly defined learning areas: blocks, sand table, reading area, listening center, dramatic play area, computers, writing area, science table, and so forth. Boundaries for these areas can be created by placing furniture in strategic ways to provide large divided areas for groups. If space is limited, the same effect can be created by placing carpets or carpet squares to indicate learning areas. You can also use hula hoops or even colored duct tape to assign an area for students to gather around and work with materials in a cooperative way.

- There should be areas for both active and quiet learning experiences. Quiet areas may need to be partitioned off in a corner or placed in an area out of high-traffic use, yet they should be visible to the teacher at all times. Many times teachers will create "caves" or "igloos" that children can climb into with books and friends. While these areas are *very* popular with kids—it is undeniably fun—problems occur when the teacher is not able to see what is going on in the tent or enclosed area. Having an area where you cannot see the children at all times is like not supervising them at all. There are alternatives to enclosed quiet areas. Try hanging an arbor above the reading area and decorate it with garland celebrating the season. Complete the "secret garden" with large throw pillows and a small carpet or rug to create an inviting place for kids to enjoy their favorite books or to work quietly. The arbor provides the illusion of a special quiet area without obstructing the teacher's view. (See the Resources in the back of this book for more information about making a reading arbor.)

- Materials and learning manipulatives should be easily accessible to the students. In order to maximize the functionality of the classroom, students should be able to get the materials they need without adult assistance. This enables students to take ownership for their learning, become more independent, and participate as valued members of the learning community. Students benefit from the opportunity to initiate their own learning activities and interact with their classmates. The teacher will, of course, have procedures in place to monitor the appropriate materials, needs, interests, and learning experiences. But there should be school supplies and materials readily available to students for times when creativity and problem solving spontaneously occur. Allowing students access to materials and manipulatives also provides them with the security that they are valued members of the learning community, that the materials belong to all of them. The procedures in place will reinforce the proper use of the materials.

- Take into account high-traffic areas: sinks, drinking fountains, restrooms, storage areas, closets, and areas where students get supplies or put finished work. If you have students who are easily distracted, do not make their permanent seating arrangement near these areas. If you decide to do flexible seating arrangements where the students are allowed freedom to choose where they will sit, you will want to discuss with the student seating options so the child can make a good choice. When the teacher provides opportunities for children to make meaningful choices, including whether to participate in small-group activities or work alone, he or she promotes the development of good problem solving strategies and reasoning.

- A large, unobstructed area should be made available for large-group activities and movement. It is not uncommon in kindergarten classrooms to have a large carpeted area for times when music, movement, and games become part of the learning experience. This area often becomes the focal point in the classroom, where the class gathers to learn, share, and create meaningful relationships.

- Students should have easy access to the teacher and instruction when they are seated at tables. Objects, furniture, and equipment should not block their view, and students should have a straight view to the instruction or demonstration. If the children are seated around a table and some of them have their backs to the instructional area, the teacher can call for "learning chairs," a signal to students who are facing in the wrong direction to turn their chairs around so they can see the teacher. This is a simple solution that takes very little practice.

- The room should be aesthetically appealing. While this may sound frivolous, an environment that is unpleasant to work in will not be conducive to good work. Creating a work space that allows for lots of natural light, live plants, and welcoming areas for both quiet and active learning is important. These spaces should also exhibit the children's work and evidence that it is truly a learning environment. These spaces should include comments from the students as learners, photographs to remind children of past learning and projects as well as lists of things yet to be learned.

Think About This . . .

What are some possible distractions in your classroom that could prevent students from learning? Can you identify the high-traffic areas in your classroom? How are high-traffic areas handled? Is there sufficient space? Are students who are attention challenged seated near these areas? Are there clear and distinct learning areas? How can you arrange your classroom in a way that will minimize distractions, provide ease and fluid movement, and maximize learning opportunities? Is there ample room for special equipment for students with physical disabilities? Are the areas for paint, sand, water, and clay placed in a location for easy clean up? Are computers placed near walls where wires and surge protectors are out of the way of traffic?

Classroom Learning Environment

Obviously, an appropriate and supportive environment for kindergarten children does not involve only the room arrangement but also the learning that happens in the room and the value placed upon that learning. According to The National Association for the Education of Young Children, or NAEYC, young children learn best in an environment where they "function as a community of learners in which all participants consider and contribute to each other's well-being and learning" (1997). This environment is built through positive and supportive relationships both among the students and with the adults who care for them every day. These relationships are established by having conversations with both the students and their families to develop a rich understanding of the child's prior learning experiences, interests, and home culture. When the teacher integrates pieces of this information into the work designed for the students, the learning experiences will be more meaningful and the students will feel valued, safe, and respected. They will in turn learn to value and respect the differences in others.

The development of social relationships is very important to the framework of learning. When children interact in work and play situations and have regular opportunities to converse, create, and problem solve together, their learning is enhanced by the sharing of varied perspectives and personal experiences. The students learn not only the academic concepts designed by the teacher but tolerance and understanding for the opinions and views of others. How the teacher structures classroom procedures, as well as how he or she models these processes on a daily basis, ultimately determines the success of the learning community.

Of course, for any learning to take place, the learning community must be a safe place. It must be physically safe, and it must be a place where ideas are valued and risk-taking is respected. Everyone desires a working environment where he or she is free of ridicule and where unsuccessful attempts are not considered failures but rather learning experiences. Ensuring that students feel relaxed and comfortable and meeting their physiological needs, such as fresh air, proper nutrition, and a balance between activity and rest, will reap benefits in maximum learning.

Role of Curriculum and Instructional Practices

When creating a safe and engaging learning community, the teacher uses pedagogical knowledge as well as knowledge about individual students to develop and organize learning opportunities for the children where they will have time to explore their world and make connections between it and the content learned in the classroom. Often when the words *explore* or *discover* are uttered to kindergarten teachers, they conjure up images of free play (which sometimes translates into wasted time) and missed opportunities to teach the standards. It is important to understand that the standards and developmentally appropriate practices are not mutually exclusive. When the standards are investigated thoroughly and compared to developmentally appropriate practices as outlined by the NAEYC, it is clear that most state standards fit into that category.

The problem begins when teachers feel pressured to conform to more traditional modes of instruction such as workbooks, worksheets, and seatwork. While these resources are not bad, and often can reinforce concrete activities, they are just resources and should not be the focal point of instructional opportunities. Young children are active learners and need to relate as many sensory experiences as possible to each new concept. During these learning experiences, students need to make predictions, solve problems, ask questions, reflect upon their findings, and discuss what they know and what they have learned with others. The standards, as illustrated in the Classroom Snapshots, require students to do all of these things and more.

Developmentally Appropriate Practices and the Standards

One concern voiced by administrators and others is that developmentally appropriate practices mean that students will just float endlessly and never be challenged to grow. This is a myth that needs to be eliminated. Kindergarten teachers know that while much of what a young child does in school is play, it is through those playful activities that development and understanding takes place. Many traditional kindergarten experiences such as sand and water play, dramatic play, art, blocks, and cooking are being discarded in an effort to make kindergarten look more like the rest of the school. But inappropriate instruction in kindergarten does not make a stronger first-grader. As a matter of fact, the reverse is more likely to occur.

Without necessary and developmentally appropriate concrete experiences, the child does not acquire the necessary foundations for future learning. The learning-centered classroom provides these experiences for all students and takes them from where they are to the expectations of the state standards and frequently beyond.

The teacher's constant monitoring and assessing of the students provides him or her with the information necessary to adjust and modify the learning activities to meet the needs of each child. Whether the child is struggling, on target, or exceeding the state expectations, it is the teacher's responsibility to ensure all students are learning and not just completing mindless or redundant work. The teacher's expectations should be high for all students. It is true that there will be some students who are developmentally delayed, and the teacher will make adjustments as needed for these children. The developmentally delayed child will still show growth from the beginning of the year to the end and be a little closer to the first-grade expectations than when he or she started. If the delay is significant, the Response to Intervention process will require that the teacher, parent, and other professionals to work together to make the appropriate decisions about how to proceed.

Cooperative Grouping Strategies

One highly successful modification is cooperative grouping. This is not a new idea; kindergarten teachers have been grouping students together since the beginning of kindergarten. What may not be a part of the equation is how the students are grouped and the activities that occur while the students are grouped. Spencer Kagan developed over one hundred cooperative learning structures, or learning strategies, where students work with their peers to organize their thinking, to think more creatively, and to learn to problem solve. Most of the structures are flexible enough to work with many concepts and topics. Kagan has written many books about these structures. A few are summarized below.

- **Corners:** This activity requires the students to represent their point of view by physically moving to a designated area of the room. Many kindergarten teachers play a game called color corners, which is a variation of this game. To align it with academic standards, the teacher announces the topic and choices, indicating which corner is designated for each choice. After having a short amount of time to think silently, the students are allowed to walk to the corner that corresponds with their answer. They do not discuss their choice with anyone else. Once they are in their corner, the children find a partner with whom to discuss the reason for their choice. The teacher allows a representative from the group to share.

- **Formations:** This is an excellent activity for students who are kinesthetic learners. The object of the activity is for the students to create the shape of the letter, object, or number called out by the teacher. The students are grouped, and the teacher announces that they will work as a team to decide how they will form the letter, object, or number. All students must participate in the decision making process as well as the formation of the assignment. Once the team has decided what to do, they physically make the formation.

- **Think-pair-share:** Many kindergarten teachers use this strategy as well. The students are allowed to think quietly about a question posed by the teacher. After a few seconds, the students find a partner and share their ideas. After a few minutes, the pairs share their ideas with the whole group, thus providing the students with an opportunity to develop communication skills as well as the ability to reflect before answering questions, which is great for developing reasoning skills.

These strategies are just a sample of activities that provide the students with varied and novel learning experiences. They provide the child with choices and the opportunity to problem solve alone and with peers. It is through these types of activities that students stay motivated and interested in completing assignments.

Technology in the Classroom

Technology provides another avenue for introducing novelty and interest into the curriculum. There has been controversy over the appropriateness of using technology with young children, some concerns being that the use of computers and other technology would substitute real experiences with virtual ones. The fear that students would be "plugged in" and miss out on important foundational activities seems to dominate. In 1996, the NAEYC released their position on the use of technology in the classroom, stating that when used responsibly and appropriately, technology—specifically computers—can benefit young children. As with all instructional tools, teachers need to assess how technology can enrich, reinforce, and support the developmentally appropriate activities supplied in the classroom.

When coupled with children's enjoyment of computer use and improved educational value in software, technology becomes an effective means for extending learning. It engages children in creative play and problem solving as well as develops concept understanding and an enthusiastic exchanging of ideas. Contrary to traditional beliefs, social interaction is increased through the use of computers, as young children prefer to work in small cooperative groups to seek help and interact in higher levels of communication than during traditional activities (Clements, Nastasi, & Swaminathan, 1993).

NAEYC recommends that technology become a regular part of the learning environment, incorporated into the teacher's already well-planned curriculum and used to enhance it. Easing technology into the learning-centered classroom takes just a few steps:

- place computers in the classroom;
- allow students daily access to computers;
- choose software that provides the students with interactive ways to connect with the concepts taught; and
- integrate the technology across content areas.

Such strategies will provide the students opportunities to stretch their thinking, to enrich their learning activities with concrete manipulatives, and to make conceptual connections.

In the Classroom Snapshot that follows, Mr. Goodwin demonstrates how he provides appropriate learning-centered activities for his students that include the integration of technology to enhance and develop the concept of graphing.

Classroom Snapshot—Mr. Goodwin Lesson: Integrating Technology Into the Curriculum

The Standards

Math: Probability and Statistics. The student constructs and uses graphs of real objects or pictures to answer questions. The student is expected to construct graphs using real objects or pictures in order to answer questions and use information from a graph of real objects or pictures in order to answer questions.

Math: Underlying Processes and Mathematical Tools. The student applies kindergarten mathematics to solve problems connected to everyday experiences and activities in and outside of school. The student is expected to select or develop an appropriate problem solving strategy including drawing a picture, looking for a pattern, systematic guessing and checking, or acting it out in order to solve a problem and use tools such as real objects, manipulatives, and technology to solve problems.

Math: Underlying Processes and Mathematical Tools. The student communicates about kindergarten mathematics using informal language. The student is expected to explain and record observations using objects, words, pictures, numbers, and technology and relate everyday language to mathematical language and symbols.

Math: Underlying Processes and Mathematical Tools. The student uses logical reason to make sense of his or her world. The student is expected to reason and support his or her thinking using objects, words, pictures, numbers, and technology.

Technology: Solving Problems. The student uses appropriate computer-based productivity tools to create and modify solutions to problems. The student is expected to use software programs with audio, video, and graphics to enhance learning experiences; and use appropriate software, including the use of word processing and multimedia, to express ideas and solve problems.

The Lesson

Mr. Goodwin has a typical heterogeneous class of kindergarten students in a highly mobile community. He frequently uses technology to enrich and reinforce concepts taught in the classroom. He is aware of the controversy that surrounds the issue of computer use in the early childhood classroom, but he ensures that the students are provided with many hands-on and interactive experiences in the classroom. He views the computer as another instructional tool and not a substitute for real experience. His students go to the computer lab once a week to create

pages for class books or other projects. In addition, there are three older computers in his classroom that he uses for computer games, interactive listening centers, and Web sites that reinforce skills.

In today's lesson, the students are going to the computer lab to create a turkey glyph that will be used during a graphing activity. A glyph is a visual method of collecting personal data about the students in order to use in graphing (please see the Resources in the back of this book for an example). The students respond to personal questions, and depending upon how they answer, the picture they create is formed. For instance, in this activity, the students will color a turkey, which will become part of a bulletin board learning center. Mr. Goodwin's first question is about the age of the student. The child is to answer the question and use the corresponding color for the turkey's head: if the student is five, the color they choose is red; if they are six, they choose orange. (See Resources for glyph directions.) After the entire glyph is created, the turkeys will be printed in color, laminated, and used in the graphing activities at the beginning of the math lessons for the rest of the week.

It is the second nine weeks, and the children are familiar with the behavioral expectations and procedures for using the computers as well as the drawing program they will be using. In this lesson, the kids listen carefully and follow directions; fortunately, there is an instructional assistant in the lab at all times to help assist and monitor the students. The students are familiar with glyphs, but this is the first time they have created one on the computer.

Mr. Goodwin says, "All right boys and girls, today we are going to make turkey glyphs on the computer. You will need to be good listeners because I am going to ask you four questions. You will not color your turkey by selecting your colors like before. The answers to the questions will tell you what color to use. Since I know that you like choosing your own colors, I have printed out some of the blank turkeys for you to paint in the classroom this week. So please be honest with your answers so we can use them when we graph this week."

Mr. Goodwin continues the lesson by asking each question and pausing to allow students to respond by filling in the corresponding part of the turkey picture. The teacher and instructional assistant monitor the students and make sure all students have completed the task before moving on to the next question. Mr. Goodwin reminds the students that when they have finished filling in the color, they should put their hands in their laps. One child raises her hand and asks for help because she had somehow deleted the color she put on the turkey. The students work in pairs with each child having his or her own computer but working together for assistance and clarification when necessary. Soon the class is finished with the lesson. The assistant and Mr. Goodwin help the students to save their work to a folder on the server so the turkeys can be printed out later. Then they go back to the classroom.

The following day, Mr. Goodwin gathers the children around on the carpet. In the center of the carpet is a long sheet of bulletin board paper with a line down the middle. At the top he has written "How old are we?" He gives each child their glyph and proceeds with part two of the lesson.

Mr. Goodwin says, "Yesterday we made glyphs on the computers. Today we are going to use the glyphs to graph the first question. We will use these every day this week and graph each of the four questions. We will learn a lot from each other as well as learning how to create and gain information from a graph. You were to complete this sentence: I am _____ years old. If you are five, you were to color the turkey's head red. If you are six years old, you were to color the turkey's head orange. Before we make our graph, let's predict how many students we think are five. Raise your hand if you have a number you think is close." He calls on students and asks for their prediction as well as a reason for why they chose the number. He also records their answers on the chart.

Jasmine: My number is twenty. I picked twenty because I think most of the kids in the room are five.

Mr. Goodwin: How many children are there in our class?

Jasmine: Twenty-two, but there may be somebody who is six.

Mr. Goodwin: That sounds reasonable. Good work! Jason, what do you think?

Jason: I think everybody is five, so I pick twenty-two.

Mr. Goodwin: So you do not think that anyone is six?

Jason: Right.

Mr. Goodwin continues around the circle until everyone has an opportunity to predict and justify an answer. He then asks students with a red-headed turkey to place their turkeys in the column on the right. At the bottom of the graph he writes "Number of children who are five." He then has the remaining students place their turkeys on the graph. The students count the eighteen red turkeys together.

Ana: I guessed it right! I guessed it right!

Mr. Goodwin: Very good, Ana! You must know a lot about our class. Here's a first-grade question for all of you: If we have eighteen students in the class who are five, how many children are six? Before you tell me your answer, tell me how we can find out the answer.

Elise: We could count the orange turkey heads.

DeAndre: We could count backwards from twenty-two. That would give us the answer.

Mr. Goodwin: Those are both really good ideas. DeAndre, how does counting backward help us find the answer?

DeAndre: Because we have twenty-two kids in our room. If we count backward to eighteen, we would be able to find out how many kids are not five.

Mr. Goodwin: We need to try out those ideas. Before we do, does anyone else have an idea of how to find the answer?

Mr. Goodwin continues to take suggestions and has the students test their ideas using the graph. After the lesson is over, the students record the results on graph paper,

 writing the words and coloring in one block for each turkey. The teacher collects the turkeys and the recording sheets. He then creates a bulletin board. On the board he displays the key and questions for the glyphs, the students' turkeys and recording sheets, as well as an index card that states "WE LEARNED: _____" with the standards listed.

Reflection on the Classroom Snapshot

Learning computer skills is a part of the state standards Mr. Goodwin must follow, but he uses those standards as a way to support other academic standards which he meets using developmentally appropriate practices. He combines the meaningful and engaging computer activities with the concrete manipulation of the glyphs to reinforce the graphing activities. These activities help to build the classroom community by revealing commonalities within the members of the class and providing opportunities for enthusiastic conversations.

Creating the glyphs on the computer provides important communication and listening skills, as well as building necessary computer skills. After the glyphs are created, the students use them as manipulatives to solve problems relating to the learning community.

Pulling It All Together

When creating a learning-centered classroom, the teacher

- creates a physical learning environment that fosters growth;
- encourages cooperative learning opportunities;
- uses technology as a tool to enrich and reinforce developmentally appropriate practices and state standards;
- provides varied and novel activities for students;
- allows students to make choices to facilitate ownership in learning; and
- continually assesses and monitors student development and growth in order to provide support and modifications to maximize learning.

Reflection . . .

- What do I do to ensure learning for every child?
- Do I provide varied and novel activities for my students?
- How do I integrate technology into my curriculum?
- How can I improve the quality of cooperative learning activities provided to my students?

Key 6

Recognize Your Students as Members of Families, Communities, and Sociocultural Groups

I note the obvious differences between each sort and type, but we are more alike, my friends, than we are unalike.

—Maya Angelou

Culture

A teacher of a learning-centered classroom creates an environment where the respect for and connections to racial, cultural, linguistic, and class backgrounds are essential for successful learning to take place. The teacher incorporates appropriate and responsive strategies that respect the children's home culture and learning styles. These strategies provide daily and consistent opportunities for the children to gain a daily appreciation and understanding of each other's diverse lifestyles—not just for the holidays or specified units.

What is culture? There is a great deal of discussion about the cultural background and heritage of different groups in our country and whether schools are meeting the diverse needs of these groups. Multitudes of studies and volumes of literature have been written about the inconsistent and unequal treatment of children from diverse backgrounds. It is so important that legislators have mandated multicultural awareness be embedded into the general curriculum. So, what is culture? To answer that question, you must ask yourself this: What makes you unique? Is it your gender, race, ethnicity, religion, occupation, geographic location, disability, or economic status? Some would argue it is all of the above. Each element influences how you view and respond to the world around you. How you live your daily life according to experiences from each of these elements, including your traditions and values, is your home culture. The common views and experiences you have with others from any of the individual groups—race, gender, religious, etc.—become your cultural background and identity.

In her book *How to Teach Students Who Don't Look Like You*, Bonnie Davis suggests that educators must "examine their own culture" first to see how it influences their view and judgments of events and others (2006, p. 3). It is through understanding why *you* look at the world in a certain way that you can then begin to look at the world from another perspective. By asking a *few* simple questions, you can see how your viewpoints may color your assumptions about the diversity of your students and how they learn. For example, ask yourself these questions: How important is multicultural education? How often should multicultural or diversity content be presented? What is an appropriate way to approach sensitive content when the topic arises? Do I view the multicultural material in my curriculum as another thing to check off a to-do list? How does my culture influence how I present the material? How do I pay respect to the home cultures of my students?

Davis suggests that teachers describe themselves in order to think about the "hidden rules" related to their culture groups (Payne, 1996, p. 9). These hidden rules can mean the difference between success and failure for students (and adults) when they try to enter a different cultural environment. It might be as simple as a matter of eye contact when speaking to an adult or the volume of a voice. For a teacher of middle-class background, making eye contact when speaking is an issue of respect, whereas for a child of poverty, it may be disrespectful to look into the eyes of an authority figure. The same can be true of voice quality. For a child of poverty, especially if there are several siblings, using a loud voice inside could be the way the child gets heard. He or she may be unaware that the volume is too loud for the classroom. It is important for the teacher to be aware of these differences so the child is not penalized for not knowing the hidden rules. When the teacher acquires a new understanding of the world through gained cultural information, he or she can begin to make the modifications necessary for the students to connect with the content and skills and their peers at a deeper level.

Include Families and Caregivers

It is common practice for teachers of young children to solicit caregivers to volunteer in the classroom or assist on field trips. It is not uncommon to have family members come to the classroom to share work related or life experiences with the students, but these are usually on special occasions. It is critical, however, in a learning-centered classroom to go further in the effort to involve parents and caregivers in the educational process (Gaitan, 2004; Powers, 2005; Prior & Gerard, 2007). When parents and caregivers are given an opportunity to collaborate with teachers on issues such as literature, curriculum, and instructional strategies, the teacher is given the information necessary to modify the curriculum such that it will meet the needs of all students.

Classroom Snapshot—Ms. Macrone
Lesson: All About Me

State Standards

Social Studies: Geography. The student understands the concept of location. The student is expected to use terms including over, under, near, far, left, and right to describe relative locations and locate places on the school campus and describe their relative locations.

Social Studies: Geography. The student understands the physical and human characteristics of the environment. The student is expected to identify human characteristics of places such as types of houses and ways to earn a living.

Social Studies: Economics. The student understands that basic human needs are met in many ways. The student

is expected to identify basic human needs and explain how basic human needs of food, clothing, and shelter can be met.

The Lesson

It is 8:15 a.m. and the students are lined-up outside the classroom, eager to begin their day. Ms. Macrone is standing at the door, smiling and greeting each one with a pat on the back and "Good Morning! How are you today?" The children look up and smile at her; some give a quick hug and then move into the classroom to put away their belongings. Ms. Macrone's classroom is filled with evidence of the very diverse learners who occupy it—cultural artifacts from the students' homes, posters, and a multicultural word wall.

The children go to the carpet and sit down for the morning routine. Every day the children sit in a circle and tell about something they experienced since they saw each other last. Some share what they had for dinner, others discuss games they played or something they saw on the way to school. If they are feeling sad or upset, this is a time when they can share those feelings as well. This is a safe place, and the children and teacher respect feelings of all kinds in this room.

After all of the students have an opportunity to share, Ms. Macrone announces that today they will be taking a walk in the neighborhood. This is something they do on a regular basis. Today, the children will look at their houses. Most of the children live within a few blocks of the school, so they are all aware of where their classmates live. The focus today is the neighborhood itself. The students are going to draw a map of the neighborhood around their home with special attention to yard art. The final assessment will be a drawing of their home and the houses on their street.

Several parents have volunteered to assist during the walk. Ms. Macrone provides each student with a clipboard, some paper, and a pencil just prior to the journey. Then she instructs the students, "Use your eyes to remember details of what you see in your neighborhood. We will stop by each house and talk about what we see.

You will then be able to make a quick drawing of what you see."

As the children walk down the street, they excitedly begin pointing to their houses and to objects found in the neighborhood. Some houses are painted bright colors, others have holiday decorations in the yard, and still others have stone sculptures of turtles, frogs, or other animals near a small waterfall. There are many topics of conversations along the way—students notice that some homes have pets in the backyard, and others have yards that are very lavishly landscaped—which inspire the young artists to draw hurriedly before they move on to the next house.

Ms. Macrone shows the children how a simple map looks. "It's like we are flying above the houses. We can see everything below us," she explains. She models by showing the children a satellite picture of the school she has downloaded from the Internet and then drawing a map on chart paper. Ms. Macrone then has the students list the things they remember from their walk while she makes a chart listing the items and drawing a small picture to go with each word. One of the mothers writes the Spanish word next to the English version and pronounces it to the children, having them repeat it after her. Finally the children go to their table and draw their map, bilingual key included.

Reflection on the Classroom Snapshot

Throughout the year, Ms. Macrone makes connections and builds relationships with her students and their families. These connections are evident in her classroom from the way she incorporates the home culture into the curriculum. She further demonstrates her respect for her students' families by inviting family members into the classroom, using the caregivers as a resource for translation of words from English to Spanish and sharing their cultural stories and experiences with the entire class. The respect she shows the families is reciprocated by the effort and respect they show to her, and their willingness to work with her benefits all the students.

These benefits are evident when the parents who volunteered to assist during the neighborhood walk act as caring adults. They listen to the students' ideas and thoughts about the homes, and they provide assistance to the children when they are drawing their maps. The parents offer further support by helping students as they complete their maps in the classroom and label the keys in both English and Spanish. The neighborhood walk, while possible without the aid of the parents, would not have been as rich or as meaningful of an experience.

Strategy: Communicate with families.

In a learning-centered classroom, communication is a paramount element for success. All families have distinct differences in home cultural values and beliefs, and it is the teacher's responsibility to support the families as well as the students. It is through effective communication that this support is accomplished, even when linguistic differences are present.

If the family is bilingual, a sensitive effort should be made to ensure all written correspondence sent home is in the home language as well as in English. Even when family members speak English, it is not guaranteed that they will have the same comprehension level with written communications such as newsletters (see Resources at the end of this book for examples), permission notes, invitations for parent conferences, school events, and report cards. Educators often use words that are part of the school culture when they send school communications to families. Special effort should be made to clarify any of these terms, including acronyms, to ensure family members and caregivers understand what is being communicated.

The same consideration and effort should be made during face-to-face meetings with families. Prior to the meeting, ask the caregiver if he or she would like an interpreter present. This person can be a school employee who is familiar with the procedures and culture of the school environment and therefore can provide background information as well as translating the conversation between teacher and caregiver. Be sensitive to the family's schedule as well. Meetings during regular business hours at school may not be convenient or possible for the caregiver. Providing the caregiver with options, such as meeting on Saturday or in the evening at home, can show that you care about and value the family's participation in their child's education. It also shows a willingness to include them and their home culture in your classroom and your curriculum.

If you meet with the family in their home, use the home language. If you do not speak the home language, let the family know that you will be bringing an interpreter with you. Respect the home culture and customs as well as the family's schedule—parents with many children may need to make the meeting short in order to care for the children. If the caregivers work outside of the home, be sensitive to the time limitations their work schedules place on them. Meal preparation and other daily routines may still need tending to and you will be taking up part of that time.

Strategy: Create a culturally sensitive learning-centered classroom.

Culturally sensitive classrooms are created by allowing elements from the home culture into the classroom to provide rich experiences and awareness for all students. It is not uncommon for kindergarten teachers to provide time for students to share their home lives with their school friends; show-and-tell is one such practice. The teacher can take a more culturally focused approach to this practice by allowing the students to bring a favorite item from home to share and explain why the item is of special significance, or to bring a family picture and share the story behind the picture.

Home culture can be brought into the classroom by highlighting a student each week. A teacher can provide a "Superstar Student" bulletin board in the classroom where a selected student brings pictures and items to share with the class that reflects who they are and their values. The child's family can participate by creating a poster that further illustrates what is important in their home culture. The teacher should be sensitive to the economic constraints of the students' families and provide materials, if necessary. The teacher can allow students to create a class book to be presented to the superstar at the end of the week. The pages would describe something their classmates respect or admire about the featured student. (See the Resources in the back of this book.)

Strategy: Bridge cultural barriers.

Helping to bridge cultural barriers in the learning-centered classroom includes providing support to the family and home culture. Some cultural barriers may not be of a linguistic nature. The caregivers may speak English, but have not had the educational opportunities necessary to help their child with homework or assist their child in areas of need. This may be a very sensitive issue, especially if the caregivers mistrust school officials. Building a trusting relationship will help, but the caregivers need to know that the teacher will not judge them. Providing opportunities that show you value their cultural differences will foster this relationship. Hosting a Family Potluck Night where families bring a favorite cultural dish to share is just one idea for such an opportunity. Community service projects, such as a school beautification venture where families and students create a mural depicting cultural values or a community garden where families and neighbors participate in the clean up, preparation, and cultivation of a garden for the community, are also good vehicles for bridging cultural barriers. There are often grant opportunities to provide funds for such projects.

Schoolwide events could include a Cultural Oral History Night where family members share historical events and the cultural signif-icance of these events. An author study, where the school links and integrates books from a single author to the core curriculum, is another possibility. Each student is given a copy of the author's book with the culminating activity being a meal for the families where the author shares his or her inspiration for writing as well as important information about reading to children. While this can be quite costly, community businesses are often willing to support such events and school and community grant opportunities are available.

Strategy: Support caregivers.

Encourage your students' caregivers and provide them with the tools they need to reinforce what you are teaching their child in class. Many times, the lack of participation and response to communication (homework, notes from the teacher, etc.) is due to a lack of under-standing. Parents with limited educational opportunities may not understand what the teacher is asking the child to do or may not have the confidence (especially in a personally difficult subject) to assist their child at home. Provide learning opportunities for caregivers by sharing strategies for helping their child with homework and study habits and providing interactive Web sites and technical support.

Pulling It All Together

When creating a learning-centered classroom, the teacher

- respects and values the cultural differences and similarities of each family;
- integrates the home culture of the students as part of an enriching experience for all;

- welcomes family input about literature, curriculum materials, and practices; and
- builds relationships through mutual respect.

Reflection . . .

- Have I solicited information from caregivers in order to better understand their child and the home culture?
- How well do I address the cultural differences of my students?
- Do I incorporate cultural differences into the curriculum daily?
- How do students perceive my body language?
- Do I model what I expect from students?

Key 7

Establish Partnerships With Students and Families

The family unit plays a critical role in our society and in the training of the generation to come.

—Sandra Day O'Conner

Building Relationships

Effective and meaningful teacher-caregiver relationships are a key feature of learning-centered kindergarten teaching. Families send their children to school with the highest of expectations—they expect the best educational experiences provided by the best teacher. This level of educational excellence can only occur if the teacher and caregiver work together. Assuming that the responsibility for establishing and maintaining these partnerships belongs to the teacher, many strategies must be used for initiating and maintaining contact as well as building relationships with the families of all students (Lawrence-Lightfoot, 2003).

The plan begins with the teacher contacting the family before the first day of school. Once the teacher obtains the class list, an effort should be made (by either mail or phone) to welcome the child and family as members of the learning community. An invitation to school before the official first day is a good way to answer any questions the family may have, alleviate the child's anxiety, and provide the family members an opportunity to share information about their child. This single act will also help the child make a connection with you, the caring, considerate teacher. It also lets the caregivers know that you value them as an advocate for their child and that the information they have to share with you is, of course, valuable and will help make the year more enjoyable and beneficial for everyone.

Once the school year begins, include caregivers whenever possible on the decision making process. Allow them to preview literature or curriculum materials and share their opinions. They may be able to suggest better examples that you may find helpful when creating lessons for the class. Pay close attention to the impact race, class, language, and culture has on the classroom and the teacher-caregiver partnerships. This is not suggesting that you allow caregivers to take over the lesson planning process, but rather that you use their suggestions to gain valuable insights into other cultures and incorporate them into the daily experiences of all the students. If you are from the majority culture, you may be surprised how differently someone else may view the materials that you feel are innocent and harmless. These differences can bring richness to the learning experiences and provide the support necessary for all children to learn—every day, no exceptions—and mutual trust is gained when you show respect to the information gained from the caregiver.

Go the Extra Mile

Depending upon the cultural influences in your school community, some caregivers may feel uncomfortable coming to the school building. Often, caregivers feel this way because their memory of school conjures up negative feelings or their childhood experiences were not happy ones. Some caregivers may not understand the importance of their role and participation in their child's education, looking to the teacher as the expert. In either case, these caregivers may resist coming to conferences or school events, responding to newsletters and notes from the teacher, or helping with school projects. Although it is tempting for a frustrated teacher to assume the caregiver just doesn't want to be bothered, this is usually not the case. Caregivers probably want to help but may feel out of their element or frustrated when they are unsuccessful in assisting their child, perhaps because they are using practices they remember from when they went to school.

These challenges can sometimes be remedied by literally going the extra mile to meet the caregivers where they are. Calling the family to arrange a meeting at their home or a place they feel more comfortable is a wonderful way to learn about the culture of the children in your classroom. Once a standard practice, many teachers today are not comfortable meeting the families in the home. This makes meeting at the coffee shop or nearby park a way to lower the anxiety level (for both teacher and families) and make everyone feel more relaxed.

Wherever you decide to meet, the first few meetings and phone calls should be spent asking the caregivers' opinions, seeking information about their child, and showing them how much you value what they have to say. Make a list of *positive* comments to share about their child—the family needs to know that you see what they see. Once the trust relationship has been established, you will be able to work on the areas of concern together. Continue to send positive comments and compliments throughout the year. This is easily done by writing a "happy note," a short, positive comment accompanied by a smiley face on a sticky note or other fun notepaper, and placing it on the student's paper.

Caregiver Education

Part of the relationship process is caregiver education, which can take many forms: educating caregivers about their child's abilities and talents; educating caregivers about how to help their child be more successful; or helping caregivers receive the educational assistance they may need to be successful. As with your classroom students, the information and activities you provide need to be based upon the knowledge you have gleaned from having conversations and interactions with the caregivers. As a trusted professional, you will know what their interests are and the most appropriate way to present the information. For instance, if your students come from an affluent community, organizing activity bags that include the book *The Gingerbread Man*, prepared gingerbread cookie dough, and cookie cutters for the caregivers to read and bake with their children at home may not be necessary or meet the expectations of your students' home cultures.

Educating caregivers about their child's abilities and talents is the most common form of caregiver education and your first responsibility. There should be a constant and consistent stream of conversation between the teacher and the family throughout the year. One way to guarantee a confrontation with an angry caregiver is to keep a child's academic weakness "a secret" until the grading period ends. Caregivers do not like surprises, and rightfully so. All caregivers want their child to have success in school, and the only way they can help is if they know there is a problem. You can communicate this sort of information by simply sending home weekly progress reports or speaking briefly when the caregiver brings or picks up the child. Keeping the lines of communication open can keep families aware of any issues that may need their attention.

Educating families on the best ways to assist their children is another way to help caregivers. This can be a bit trickier, especially if the bonds and relationships have not already been established. Teachers have a wide variety of ways to accomplish this, including sending home suggestions for activities to do at home (as well as the materials, if necessary) and having afterschool make-it-and-take-it sessions providing information and activities caregivers can use with their child. This is a good time to share the research and pedagogical knowledge as to why the experiences you provide are appropriate.

When Nothing Helps

There will be times when no matter what you try a parent may be difficult, angry, or hostile. Usually it has very little to do with you and more to do with situations beyond their control in their own lives. While it is easy to tell you not to take it personally, this can be a very uncomfortable situation as no one enjoys being yelled at or berated. If you know there are caregivers who cannot be satisfied, you may want to try some of the following:

- ask an administrator to be present during conferences;
- document meetings and stick to the topic at hand—rehashing past issues will not help;
- remain calm and listen—sometimes they just need to vent; and
- create a teacher-caregiver-student contract that clearly states what each party will do to resolve the point of conflict.

Classroom Snapshot—Mr. Bradley

Charita quietly sits alone at the housekeeping center watching the other children laughing, playing, and interacting with one another. As the student most in need and at risk, she comes to school with matted hair, dirty clothes and smelling of urine. She is developmentally far behind the other students, struggling to form complete sentences to communicate with her teacher and peers and unable to remember simple concepts from day to day, but is always first to flash the most beautiful smile. Charita is a people pleaser. While she is shy and self-conscious of her language barrier, she eagerly volunteers to help her teacher and readily picks up after other children or straightens the materials at her table. During rest time, it takes her only a few minutes to fall fast asleep, and she is the last to awaken when it is time to go home.

Her teacher, Mr. Bradley, regularly brings clean clothing for Charita to change into when she arrives at school and has the school nurse assist her in cleaning up as much as possible. After many attempts to arrange for a parent conference at school to discuss these areas of concern, Mr. Bradley finally makes arrangements to meet Charita's mother on the weekend at their home. Charita's mom is a single parent with four children—three under the age of eight—and works two jobs. Charita is the only girl and helps her fifteen-year-old brother with the youngest children and housework while he fixes dinner and does his homework when mom is at work. Mr. Bradley offers to bring pizza, as the meeting time is near dinnertime, and asks if he can bring the school counselor. Mr. Bradley

shares his concerns about Charita and lets mom know that he understands her time is valuable.

Upon arrival at the house, the teacher sees the yard in front of the small house is neatly mowed with a few toys strewn around on the porch. Charita's mother greets the teacher and counselor with the same beautiful smile as Charita—warm and inviting. The house is small but tidy. The furniture and carpet are worn but clean. The youngest children are running around the living room playing with Charita, while the oldest child is playing video games on a small television in the corner of the room. Charita runs to her teacher and gives him a big hug, obviously happy to see him on the weekend. In true helper mode, Charita shows her teacher where to place the pizza and runs to the kitchen to get paper plates.

With the family fed and mother feeling more at ease, Mr. Bradley shares the academic and developmental concerns he has about Charita. He makes sure the comments he makes are not negative, and he shares Charita's strong points as well. He sympathizes with mom, her situation, working two jobs and tells her how much he admires her dedication to her children. Then he asks how he and the school can help. Charita's mother begins to cry, obviously overwhelmed by fatigue and disbelief that someone actually cares. She begins to share the story about her family's situation.

Her husband lost his job and out of desperation deserted the family, leaving Charita's mother with four children. She took two low-paying jobs to secure a home for her family. This required her children to take on more responsibility at home, even Charita. Each child has certain chores assigned to them, and Charita helps pick up after her brothers and helps with her three-year-old brother. Mother explains that Charita sleeps with her little brother who is not potty trained and ends up soaked in urine during the night. Because Charita's mother leaves home at 5:00 a.m. to go to her first job, she is not able to ensure Charita is clean and ready for school. She relies on her oldest child to get the children ready for school. The family does not have a washer and dryer at home and does not always have the available funds for the laundromat. There are also many weekends when Charita's mom will work an additional shift and does not

have the time to go. She will hand wash many of their clothes in the kitchen sink and hang them outside to dry, but with four children, that often will not last a full week.

After listening to mother, Mr. Bradley realizes that Charita is the "little mama" while mother is at work. While the situation is not ideal, mom is doing the best that she can, wanting to be self-sufficient but struggling to keep afloat. The counselor recommends some social services, free afterschool care for the children, as well as some resources for financial assistance. She makes an appointment to meet with Charita's mother the following week so the family can receive these services as soon as possible. As the teacher and counselor walk to the car to leave, Charita's mother hugs them both, thanking them for understanding and not judging her as a bad mother.

In the weeks that follow, Charita comes to school clean and rested. While she remains behind her peers developmentally, she begins to make progress. She receives extra help during the day as well as after school, thanks to the communities in school program. Before the end of the school year, she is speaking more freely and in complete sentences as well as writing at the bottom of her pictures that she is "vre hpe" [very happy].

Reflection on the Classroom Snapshot

Mr. Bradley would not have been as successful with efforts to meet Charita's needs if he had not made an effort to connect with the mother. Listening without judgment and trying to problem solve to help the mother meet the basic needs of her children created an environment where Charita could then focus upon learning. Mr. Bradley first had to build a trusting relationship with the parent, through careful and deliberate measures—sympathetic listening, constructive and positive assistance, as well as genuine concern about his student.

Strategy: Meet caregivers where they are comfortable.

Mr. Bradley took the time and effort to meet at a convenient time for the mother away from school. He could have made no attempt to assist the parent and called child protective services for neglect, but he felt it was more important to first fully investigate the situation and see if he could help. Clearly, Charita would not thrive if she were separated from her family. Once the basic needs of the family were met, Charita was able to make progress.

Strategy: Solicit caregiver input.

Mr. Bradley listened to Charita's mother and used the information given to find practical solutions that not only benefited Charita but the entire family. What seemed to be neglect turned out to be a family in crisis, struggling to survive and in need of assistance. Using the parent input, Mr. Bradley and the counselor were able to guide the parent in the right direction. Without parent input, Mr. Bradley would have made incorrect assumptions about the mother, family, and about Charita as well.

Another case in point about the importance of caregiver input is the story of Jonathan. A gifted five-year-old, Jonathan was reading at a second-grade level and had extensive knowledge in many scientific areas upon entering kindergarten. While he had advanced intelligence, he was a normally developing five-year-old socially and emotionally, and for that reason his parents requested he stay in kindergarten rather than advancing to first grade. In an effort to accommodate both his intellectual and social needs, his teacher arranged for him to attend a leveled reading group in the first-grade class for students identified as gifted. This provided him an opportunity to work with intellectual peers and reading challenges. He was also allowed time to work on science projects and experiments with fifth-grade "buddies," who came to the primary grades to work on projects with younger students. Upon completion of his projects, he was allowed to present to his classmates what he had discovered.

Jonathan also had a younger brother who frequently needed medical attention for a rare bone disease in a hospital outside the state. When this occurred, Jonathan would miss school—a lot of school. Because of his advanced academic ability, it would have been easy to excuse his absence and allow him to simply make up the work assigned to his peers. His teacher, however, wanted him to achieve as much as possible during the year. She would communicate to Jonathan and his family numerous times a day via e-mail and phone calls while they were away, keeping them abreast of events going on at school, passing on messages from Jonathan's peers, and exchanging assignments he could complete while he was away from school.

The assignments were custom-made for Jonathan, incorporating his experiences at the hospital and dealing with a seriously ill sibling with the state standards. Jonathan was given disposable cameras to journal his experiences and was able to share with his peers through e-mail and conference calls. As part of a geometry lesson, the students designed quilt panels that were later sewn by parent volunteers and donated to the children's ward of the hospital where Jonathan's brother stayed. These experiences enriched the lives of all the students and deepened their understanding of the world around them as well as emotionally supported Jonathan and his family.

Daily communication with the family became the most important tool to ensure that Jonathan, as well as the other students, was able to learn every day—no exceptions.

Strategy: No surprises.

When building a trusting partnership with caregivers, the first and most important rule involves the importance of communication: No one likes unpleasant surprises, especially regarding their children. Teachers who take the time to build relationships with students' families through newsletters, happy notes, phone calls, e-mail, conferences, and even short conversations before or after school usually reap the benefits of students who are more successful and caregivers who are receptive and cooperative. The effort put forth in communicating reveals to caregivers that the teacher truly cares about their child and is keeping up with their progress and situation at school and at home.

Do not wait until progress reports or the end of grading periods to contact families about academic or behavioral concerns. When you contact caregivers, be sure to include some positive comments. No one wants to hear only negative things about their child. It makes them feel as if the teacher doesn't like the child or views him or her as an inconvenience. This will not help to build a trusting relationship. It also can make caregivers feel as if the teacher does not know what is going on in the classroom. Surprising them with bad news, such as a child not doing well academically, gives the caregivers the impression that you are not paying attention to their child's needs. Most caregivers are willing to give extra assistance at home if they are notified of a problem. Let families know at the first indication of a problem. The teacher and the caregivers must work as a team for the success of the student.

Pulling It All Together

When creating a learning-centered classroom, the teacher

- communicates frequently to all caregivers, relaying both positive news as well as areas of concern;
- makes a connection to families by respecting the home culture and valuing caregiver input; and
- provides a safe environment for caregivers to share information about the home situation, even if it means meeting away from school.

Reflection . . .

- How do I connect with caregivers?
- How can I communicate better with the families of my students?
- How well do I know my students? Can I list five things about their home life?
- Am I willing to go the extra mile to ensure the child's success?

Key 8

Plan Meaningful Learning Experiences to Connect Your Students to the Standards

What a child can do today with assistance, she will be able to do by herself tomorrow.

—Lev Vygotsky

Developmentally-Appropriate Practice Can Be Rigorous Too

Rigorous and challenging standards for any grade level are general learning goals designed to be age appropriate. The knowledge and skills to be mastered at each grade level are intended to reflect a degree of depth and complexity that is achievable for typically-developing children of the chronological age associated with that grade. The ability to identify one letter of the alphabet, for example, would not be considered a rigorous and challenging standard for kindergarten language arts because most children can identify and read simple words, such as *stop* or their own name, in familiar contexts when they begin kindergarten. Naming coins, on the other hand, would be considered an age-appropriate and challenging expectation which can be met through the use of playing games and cooperative learning activities and by adapting the games to meet the needs and abilities of the students. For instance, having a child pull a coin out of a sock, identify, and name it is one way for a teacher to assess and provide practice for a child. The teacher can make a simple modification of this activity by placing only two types of coins in the sock for a child who is struggling to learn them and more coins in the sock for the child who has mastered most of the coins. For a child with advanced knowledge and skills in this concept, the teacher could add the task of telling how much the coin is worth or showing an equivalent amount of money, all depending upon the child's ability and need. These activities can become learning center activities later and can be used by all children as they grow and develop. All children learning every day—no exceptions.

The standards, established by each state for implementation in all of its public schools, are not necessarily designed to reflect or respond to the many variations in developmental levels, background knowledge, prior experience, educational opportunities, skill, disposition, motivation, language, and cultural heritage found among any group of kindergarten-aged children. Ultimately, the need for kindergarten teachers to acquire and use their knowledge of their students, gathered through partnerships with children's families, is more important now than ever before.

Designing Learning Experiences for a Learning-Centered Classroom

There are numerous key features that are critical when establishing a learning-centered classroom. These features include lesson design—specifically the alignment of objectives and evaluation—instructional variety, incorporating student interest, and differentiating instruction to ensure all students are given the opportunity to learn during every lesson, every day—no exceptions. Without careful and purposeful planning, the learning experiences provided may not meet the needs of all students. Lesson planning is one of the first concepts taught to preservice teachers. Most teachers know how to plan activities for their students. This chapter will focus upon the process leading up to the planning phase and how to ensure that the developmentally appropriate practices you provide will help your students meet the state standards.

Know Your Students

When creating meaningful and engaging lessons for students, the teacher has many variables to keep in mind: the developmental and academic abilities of the students, the depth and complexity of the standard or concept to be taught, the prerequisites or prior learning experiences needed, and how the outcome will be assessed, or more directly, what the student will do to prove mastery. To effectively design work for your students, you must first thoroughly know them. By knowing the students' abilities, cultural differences, and interests, the teacher will know what activities will be engaging, the difficulty level needed, and whether any background knowledge is required before the concept is taught. In any given classroom there are a multitude of developmental levels and interests, so the teacher must be creative when selecting the learning opportunities in order to meet the needs of all students.

Information about students can be gathered in a variety of ways including caregiver or student surveys (for an example, see Resources at the end of this book), formal and informal assessments, student responses through the use of graphs and glyphs, and through daily conversations with families and caregivers and the students themselves. The qualitative data you gather from these methods can reap invaluable information about each student's learning styles, the cultural experiences that each student brings to the classroom, and each student's developmental and academic abilities. Once armed with information about the learners, the teacher can then look at the content to be taught and design lessons around the needs of the learners.

The next step is to decide what standard to teach, with the assessment in mind. While this sounds like "teaching to the test," it is really trying to decide how the achieved learning will look or how you will know that students learned the objective. To do this, the teacher must ask some important questions such as, what will the students be able to do when they have mastered this skill? How will I effectively assess this standard? What do the children need to know and experience in order to fully understand this concept? By asking these questions and participating in rich conversations about the students with colleagues, the teacher can glean best practices for his or her students from a plethora of ideas. Remember: creating the learning-centered classroom is about *all* children learning every day, every lesson. Receiving outside assistance and ideas is a smarter way to work and an excellent way to grow professionally.

Once the teacher has background knowledge of the learners, as well as an idea of the concept or skill to be taught and how it will be assessed, the teacher can then begin to look at the actual designing of the lesson and engaging activities. Phillip Schlechty shares a lesson design framework in his book *Working on the Work* (2002), where he states the design qualities that should be present when designing engaging work for students. His lesson-design framework lists attributes that can lead to more meaningful learning opportunities for students. He states that all lessons should include content and substance, organization of knowledge, clear and compelling product standards, and protection from adverse consequences for initial failures. Simply put, the teacher needs to know what he or she is teaching, organize the materials and prior learning experiences needed for success, let the kids know what is expected of them, and provide students with a safe learning environment so they will be willing to take risks.

In addition, Schlechty suggests that there are other attributes that add quality and richness to the lessons: variety and novelty, choice, affirmation, affiliation, and authenticity. These qualities are the pieces that grasp the students' attention and keep them engaged and committed to the lessons. While not specifically naming these components of lesson design in her book, *Understanding Learning: The How, the Why, the What* (2002), Ruby Payne discusses the need to provide students with materials and concepts in a format that gives meaning to their lives, and she suggests providing this information in a variety of ways. This is done by building a positive, caring relationship with the student. She indicates that the relationship is so important that it can determine whether the child's learning accelerates or doesn't occur at all.

This is where truly knowing your students is beneficial. When you know what they like, dislike, their fears, dreams, and interests, it is obvious that they matter to you. Then, as the master creator, you can weave those elements into the learning opportunities that will intrinsically keep your students motivated. Some fear that this approach to teaching will simply entertain the students, but it is more than that. It is giving the children a hook from their lives on which to catch the information you are providing them.

This is why it is so important to provide those rich experiences first—take the field trip, the walk, get out the manipulatives and artifacts for the students to explore and discover *before* you teach the lesson. Think of the questions and conversations that arise with each new experience, and for students who may have experienced it before, it adds another level to the learning opportunity. Then, when you have created a lesson and provided learning activities, you and your students can reflect back to the experience and build upon it.

Teachers can make powerful connections to the standards through the arts. In many elementary schools, with financial constraints and focus upon standardized test results, the fine arts programs—visual, music, and drama—have been all but eliminated from the curriculum. Fine arts teachers are rarely found in elementary schools, so classroom teachers are being asked to take up the slack. Most kindergarten teachers already use music, movement, role-playing, and art as an important part of their daily routine and understand the benefits of these programs. Unfortunately the concepts and approach may not be as rich as they could be—music being finger plays and songs about the alphabet, art leaning more toward crafts instead of art concepts, and the drama program hinging upon the housekeeping center or role-playing during a game. While these are fine activities and should be a part of kindergarten, the arts should be explored in more depth.

The arts are a wonderful way to enrich and expand the core concepts (math, language arts, science, and social studies) being taught in the classroom. For example, color, number, shapes, and themes can be reinforced by examining works of art. Improvisation provides a creative and fun way to develop language skills and make connections to literature. Music aids students to more easily retain facts and information as well as improving math skills. Comparing masterful works of art can provide the students with a new lens by which to view the world around them and make connections with the concepts learned.

Classroom Snapshot—Ms. Sandburg

In the following Classroom Snapshot, Ms. Sandburg is in the process of designing a lesson. As a first-year teacher, she is assigned a mentor, Ms. Stone, with whom she meets to formally plan and discuss curricular concerns. By the ninth week of the school year, Ms. Sandburg has met with all the families in an effort to find out all she can about the children and their interests and learning abilities. She has also gathered information from informal and formal

assessments, such as observing her students working, conversations about information shared in class, and assessments required by the district. As the Snapshot begins, she takes this information with her as she sits down with her mentor to discuss a science lesson she wants to teach the following week.

Collegial Conversations: Preplanning Phase

As many teachers do, Ms. Stone and Ms. Sandburg meet after school, sharing anecdotes about the day and brainstorming ideas for an upcoming kindergarten grade-level planning meeting. The meeting will focus upon the next thematic unit, *All About Me*. This unit will provide students the opportunity not only to learn about themselves and their families but to build a connection to their learning community through respect of cultural similarities and differences.

Ms. Stone begins the meeting by asking her protégé if she has concerns about any of the students in her classroom. She is aware of the data Ms. Sandburg has been collecting about her students and is interested in her findings.

Ms. Stone: So, tell me about your class.

Ms. Sandburg: I have a great class! They are such good workers and most are doing a wonderful job trying to follow the rules. Most of the children who cried the first couple of weeks have gotten into the routine and are adjusting nicely. As you know, I have been assessing my students and talking to all the families. I have such a diverse class, and the home journal pages from the families are just wonderful. Jamica's mom is from Ethiopia, and she shared stories from her childhood. She plans to come and share some artifacts from her native land. I know the kids will really enjoy that.

Ms. Stone: You know, this may be something that could be continued during the *All About Me* unit we are starting next week. Let's first take a look at the standards we will be teaching and figure out what the assessment will be, so we will know how to proceed.

Designing With the End in Mind

The two teachers take out the state standards, provided by their school district, and decide upon the following two standards:

Social Studies: Culture. The student understands similarities and differences among people. The student is expected to identify personal attributes common to all people, such as physical characteristics, and identify differences among people.

Social Studies: Culture. The student understands how people learn about themselves through family customs and traditions. The student is expected to identify family customs and traditions and explain their importance, compare family customs and traditions, describe customs of the local community.

While looking at the state standards, the teachers discuss how they would assess the students. What knowledge and skills would the students exhibit if they had mastered the standards? The first standard is asking the students to make comparisons of people by looking at physical attributes and name how they are alike or different. The second standard asks the students to compare the customs and traditions of families and discuss the importance of these customs. The teachers decided to use a creative art project as a culminating activity. The teachers conclude the meeting with several ideas to share with the other teachers in their grade level.

Designing for Students

During the grade-level meeting the teachers discuss a variety of activities that will provide the students with experiences to support the standards. The "caregiver response pages" (see Resources in the back of this book) share traditions and childhood experiences and will supply important cultural information and become a valuable resource for this unit. Through this activity, the

caregivers become a part of the learning community in the classroom as well as an important cultural resource.

The grade-level meeting consists of all six kindergarten teachers and an administrator. They discuss any assessment data gathered from the previous week, the standards to be taught for the next few weeks as well as how they will be assessed, and they collaborate on ideas for activities or projects to support the children in meeting the standards. The actual designing of lessons are left to the individual teachers, as they will need to modify and adapt the learning experiences to meet the needs of their individual students. Once the assessment has been decided upon and the teachers have each contributed ideas for learning activities, the teachers have the tools they need to design lessons for their students.

The Final Project

Ms. Sandburg created many lessons for the *All About Me* unit, using the ideas and discussion points from the grade-level meeting. The final assessment is jointly created by all grade-level teachers to maintain consistency. The assessment task allows the students to create a flower that represents important aspects of their cultural backgrounds—things that make them unique. (See this lesson and template in Resources at the back of this book.) As a result of collaborating and investigating students' learning needs and distinct home cultures, Ms. Sandburg is able to provide the students with a rich tapestry of learning experiences with all students learning every day— no exceptions.

Reflection on the Classroom Snapshot

Ms. Sandburg gained valuable information from her colleagues and was able to use that information to provide learning experiences for all her students. While the only standards investigated in the Classroom Snapshot were in social studies, Ms. Sandburg creates a cross-curricular plan for the *All About Me* unit. For example, she created a Venn diagram of the students' similarities and differences taking into account physical as well as cultural features. The success her students experience is made possible through her pre-design investigations, including knowing her students, enlisting caregiver information and support, understanding the standards, and collaborating with her peers.

Strategy: Know your students.

This cannot be stressed enough. Without having a relationship with your students and truly understanding what their lives are like, as well as what motivates them, you will design lessons that are no more than busywork. Although the students may learn something, it will not be to the depth and complexity desired by you and required by the state standards.

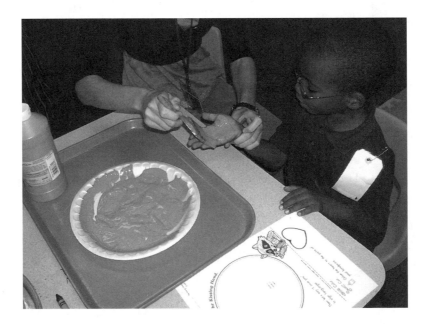

Strategy: Incorporate the family culture.

Learning about the different cultures represented in the classroom is one way to gain inside information about the students and a wonderful resource for facilitating better understanding and respect of learning and cultural differences. The family stories provide opportunities for the students to share feelings and develop an appreciation of the multicultural learning community.

Strategy: Understand the standards.

You must know the standards in order to meet the depth and complexity necessary to ensure the appropriate scaffolding is in place for student success. For a novice teacher or one new to kindergarten, collaborating with colleagues is essential to ensure the standards are being addressed in a suitable manner.

Strategy: Design with the assessment in mind.

Once the standards are understood, addressing how they will be assessed is the next step in effective lesson design. Once again, it provides the teacher with insight into the appropriate supportive instruction and experiences needed to ensure student success.

Pulling It All Together

When creating a learning-centered classroom, the teacher

- gets to know the students' likes, dislikes, abilities, interests, and home culture;
- fully understands the standards and how they will be assessed;
- collaborates with colleagues;
- uses family members as a resource to better understand home culture, traditions, and interests of the students;
- designs lessons that incorporate the data about students with activities that are presented in a variety of ways to meet their needs and interest levels; and
- continually assesses and monitors for progress and understanding.

Reflection . . .

- How well do I know my students?
- Have I obtained caregivers input in an effort to better meet the needs of their child?
- How well do I understand the standards?
- Am I teaching to the depth and complexity required by the standards?

- How do I modify and support the lessons to meet the needs of all the students and meet the state requirements?
- Do I plan with the assessment in mind?
- Do I collaborate with my colleagues?

Key 9

Showcase Your Students' Learning and Their Engagement With the Standards

There is a brilliant child locked inside every student.

—Marva Collins

Kindergarten Teachers: Really Teaching or "Just Playing"?

The life of a kindergarten teacher can be very complex and frustrating as well as challenging and rewarding. While the general public and professional peers understand that you are a bona fide teacher—fully credentialed and knowledgeable in pedagogical theory and practice—there always seems to be an underlying assumption that somehow the job of the kindergarten teacher is less stressful or valuable because there isn't a standardized test attached. Excellent kindergarten teaching often looks like "playing" to outside observers; so it becomes your responsibility as an educator to be proactive in showcasing your students' learning and in making explicit connections between the students' activities and the standards.

Throughout the country, kindergarten teachers spend endless hours designing rich and meaningful learning experiences for their students as well as communicating with students, peers, and caregivers about the needs and successes of their young scholars. But kindergarten teachers must learn to communicate more effectively about what is being done in the classroom and how it contributes to the success of the child during the "tested years." The formation of state standards came about as an effort to ensure all students were provided equal learning opportunities in preparation for the mandated state tests. Many of these standards are developmentally appropriate and easily incorporated into the daily curriculum of any kindergarten classroom. Other standards, affected by the academic shovedown, present a challenging moral dilemma for teachers who feel torn between what is developmentally best for their students and what is mandated by the state. While all children may not meet all the standards, profound and amazing learning can take place for all students—every day without exception—in your classroom. John Dewey once said, "One of the saddest things about U.S. education is that the wisdom of our most successful teachers is lost to the profession when they retire." It is perhaps sadder still if the work and wisdom of our most successful kindergarten teachers is considered to be no more than glorified babysitting. How do we ensure that the kindergarten teacher is as valued as he or she deserves? The answer: through the daily and deliberate communication by you, the teacher. The world will not know what you do unless you share its significance.

Making a Connection to the World

The more you know about the state standards and the way the rest of the school and community talks about them, the better prepared you will be when you begin sharing your work with the rest of the world. Some essential points to consider as you investigate are as follows:

- **What terminology is used in the state standards and on the upper-level tests?**
  Chances are that the same vernacular used in the standards for kindergarten is used throughout the primary and intermediate grades. Most states try to align the standards so there are few gaps in conceptual development. What is important to

remember is that kindergarten is the foundation of all future learning. Making sure you fully understand the depth and complexity of what the standard is expecting the student to learn is imperative.

- **How can you show that what your students are doing is the foundation to more complex and abstract problem solving?**
  Advertise! Share what you are doing with caregivers, the community, and colleagues. Young children cannot become problem solvers if they are never provided an opportunity to solve problems. The problems presented to the student can be simple at first (Three birds, how many legs?), but need to become more complex as the student becomes more proficient (You have thirty-five cents. If the coins are all nickels, how many nickels do you have?).

- **In what ways do you and your students connect what is being learned in the classroom with real situations in the community?**
  Field-based instruction to the local community is an excellent way to make a connection between the classroom learning community and the real-world community.

While many teachers feel they are too busy to promote what they do in the classroom, it is important to remember that without this conscious effort the community, and even upper-level peers, may continue to miss the importance of what you do. In the following Classroom Snapshot, Ms. McCardo realizes that when she made a change in her classroom, the learning community needed to understand how the work she provided her students prepared them for future academic success.

Classroom Snapshot—Ms. McCardo

Ms. McCardo is a kindergarten teacher with ten years' experience. She provides a learning-centered classroom and highly engaging and interesting learning opportunities for her students. After a grade-level book study about the Reggio Emilia schools in Italy, she decided to try some of the suggestions from the book study in her own classroom. She loved the focus of taking cues from the children's conversations about what they were interested in and using that as a source in which to generate interest for

what she needs to cover in the school and state curriculum. She also liked the way fine arts were a major player in the curriculum, a way for the children to express what they wanted to learn, how they wanted to learn it, and finally what they had learned—not just an afterthought or craft project.

She began by letting groups of children sit at tables with crayons and paper. She told them to draw anything they wanted. She explained to them that she was going to use their drawings to make plans for what they were going to learn in the weeks to come. While the children were working, she listened to their conversations, took notes, and asked questions about their drawings. She gained valuable information about what her students were interested in and data about their fine motor and verbal communication abilities, as well as their ability to process information and problem solve. Some of the children did not know how to draw the things they were interested in, some had never been asked to share an opinion and did not know how to respond to an open-ended problem. Some children thought she just wanted them to redraw something they had worked on before. She found herself wondering if they were really ready for this sort of project and if she had misunderstood what the Reggio approach was about.

After school, Ms. McCardo looks at the drawings and her documentation once again. This time she looks for patterns of concepts or topics that she could use as a way to group the children. She finds that most of the children in her classroom were interested in shapes—they drew basic shapes over and over in patterns or just randomly on the page. Some had even specifically asked to learn more about shapes and how they could use them to draw better. From this information, Ms. McCardo decided that she could use the topic of shapes for a long-term project in which she could have her students investigate other curricular topics. For instance, when the curriculum focus was upon transportation, her class used shapes to learn more about each mode of transportation. Using appliance boxes, the students created buses, boats, airplanes, and trains. The children looked at photographs of different modes of transportation and made lists of how they were

similar and different in the way they moved about, the working parts, the number of people that would be able to fit onto each type of transportation, as well as the different varieties within each group. Throughout the project, the children also compared the shapes of different modes of transportation, how the basic shapes worked together to make different 3-D shapes—such as rectangular prisms, cylinders, and cones—and how the buses, planes, boats, and cars were all made up of these geometric forms. They drew, painted, and created 3-D sculptures using a variety of mediums.

As time passed, the students remained interested in learning about geometric shapes and attributes. The students began looking at the lines of real-world objects before they would begin to draw. With each changing subtheme, such as seasons, holidays, and family, shapes were always the background topic through which they investigated the new theme. While Ms. McCardo had long-term goals and objectives for her students, she would look at the work completed by her students daily. If the students showed interest in a particular aspect of a theme or if questions came up during the day, she would allow the children's interest to dictate the direction they would go in the learning journey. She realized that regardless of which direction the children decided to go, she would be able to provide the academic requirements the state standards mandated. In fact, she found the children's interest and stamina for learning was stronger when they were able to choose the direction than when she was in "control." She also realized that she had to plan fewer activities for her students because they were deeply involved with the projects they decided to do.

As Ms. McCardo's class progressed through the long-term shape project, she realized how deeply her students were learning and she wanted to share the success with others. Normally, she would send home the work with smiley faces or stickers for parents and caregivers to discuss with their child. This time she decided she wanted the rest of the school to understand how the work she was providing for her students would be an important part of the foundation for learning success in the upper grades. She began as most teachers do, with a bulletin board of her

students' work, but soon realized the display did not portray a clear picture of the depth of learning her students had acquired in class. She realized she would have to change how she shared her students' work just as dramatically as how she now approached designing work for her students.

Ms. McCardo added signs to the bulletin board displays, explaining the project and the higher-level learning that occurred because of the learning opportunity. She also posted quotes from the students describing in their words what had been learned. This was a strategy she learned from the Reggio book study, and it was a powerful tool for letting the rest of the learning community, parents, and caregivers know that what and how the students were learning was important. It also gave the students a message that what they thought, learned, and questioned was valuable.

Soon, parents and caregivers began questioning Ms. McCardo about the project happening in her classroom. They were interested because the children would come home talking about what they had learned, using vocabulary much advanced to what they expected from five-year-olds, and excited to go to school the next day. Families wanted to be a part of the process, and Ms. McCardo was happy to have their assistance. Although she was very organized, she could always use another pair of adult hands to help with documentation, taking photos of the students working, and to write down new questions about the topics.

To help organize parents and caregivers, and to keep them abreast of what was happening in the classroom, Ms. McCardo sent home newsletters, short video documentaries on DVD—starring the students—and created a class Web page posted on the school Web site under her name. The Web page listed upcoming events for parents to attend or volunteer for, as well as the state standards and their link to the upper grades (she called it "Foundations for Future Success"). She also posted signs over the learning centers in the room. Blocks were no longer just a fun place to be, it was a learning center for developing skills in the areas of social interaction, problem solving, and spatial relationships. Anyone who entered the room could see that what appeared on the surface to be play, really had academic relevance.

Reflection on the Classroom Snapshot

In the Classroom Snapshot, Ms. McCardo used a variety of ways to advertise the depth and importance of her students' work. This effort created an opportunity for parents, caregivers, and educators alike to ask questions and value her small learners as just that—learners. It also helped clarify how what her students learned or did not learn in kindergarten would impact their performance in the upper grades and how she was preparing them to be problem solvers and thinkers for today and the future.

While Ms. McCardo re-created her classroom and the way she communicated what was happening in the learning environment, the important thing to come away from this vignette is to be brave enough to try something new. Ms. McCardo was inspired to try many aspects of the Reggio approach with her students, knowing full well that she would not be able to completely encompass the entire approach. While not mentioned in the scenario, she also rearranged her classroom to give the students more space, lowered the tables so the children could sit on the floor, and restructured the student day so they could have longer periods of time working with their project groups. It was when she realized how deeply and intensely the students were learning that she was then moved to share it with the world. The children's excitement about learning sparked a similar response in her. She was learning about how her students learn and could connect it to how they would be successful well after they left her classroom.

Many new teachers (and experienced teachers as well) feel overwhelmed by the day to day requirements and expectations from the campus, district, and state administrators. Ms. McCardo's enthusiasm may make new teachers feel inadequate, but that is not the intent of the scenario. It is, rather, to show how one teacher was able to communicate the importance and value of her students' work. If a teacher were to add even one of the suggested strategies, then it would be a step closer to making that connection to the outside world than had been made in the past. There's a lot to be said for taking it slow and easy.

Strategy: Showcase your students' work.

Many teachers are pretty good about creating bulletin boards and writing newsletters to show what the children are learning and the projects that are a result of the classroom activities. But in today's standards-focused environment, teachers need to show their communities that while they are teaching in a kid-friendly way, the work is connected to the standards. The work produced by the students should be displayed with pride in a way that shows the value and importance of what the students learn and the way they learn it. Through the use of technology, the means of communicating and the size of the audience are limited only by your imagination. Below are a few ideas for sharing the important work you and your students are doing every day.

- Create communication boards with photos of students working, examples of student products, quotes by the students about what they have learned and why, as well as how the work connects to the state standards. These displayed examples of what the children are thinking and learning can soon become a focal point for teachers, caregivers, and the community (see an example form and additional materials in the Resources at the end of this book).

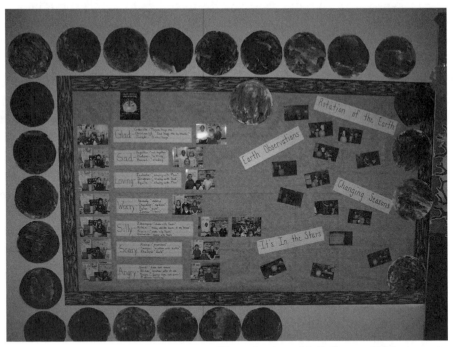

Photo by Amy McCulley and Kris Accardo

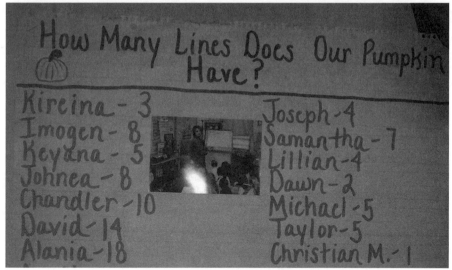

Photos by Amy McCulley and Kris Accardo

- Start an online blog site where teacher and students' families can communicate daily. This will help families to keep in touch with what is going on in the classroom and can be especially helpful to family members who may be far away, such as military parents or divorced parents who are located out of the area.

- Create videotapes or movies of students working throughout the project or study unit, including interviews with your "stars," and explaining the process and how it was valuable to them. Organize a "Film Festival" showcasing what your students have learned.

- Educate your students' families and the community by inviting them into your classroom to observe the dynamic ways the children learn. Students can act as docents of learning for your guests, sharing with them the highlights of projects past and present. The students can even be taught how to take pictures of the guests to be posted on the Web site or a communication board. Be sure to put quotes by the guests' pictures as well. Special event nights can be arranged where the families and community share in the learning through slideshows and hands-on activities to further their understanding of the importance of the students' work and its connection to the standards.

- Create a learning Web site that shares the projects and learning opportunities in your classroom. Many search engines offer free Web space and easy-to-follow directions for creating simple Web sites. Your district or campus may also have Web access for this sort of communication as well. Be sure to safeguard your students by not listing their names, and get prior permission from parents and caregivers to post photographs if the Web site goes onto the World Wide Web. An example of free Web spaces is http://www.lunarpages.com/education.php.

- Create podcasts of the projects your students have completed. When you post podcasts on your school's Web page, students, parents, caregivers, community members, and far-away relatives can see the amazing work being done by your students. Students from military families can use the podcast as verbal pen pal messages to loved ones far away to share what is going on in the classroom.

- Celebrate and showcase learning with the school, families, and the community by hosting events throughout the year. Programs, art shows, musicals, poetry slams, and living museums are just a few ways to let the world know what your students are doing is more than just play.

- Share how kindergarten students learn with other teachers. The exquisite teaching practices of kindergarten teachers are strategies that are very effective for *all* grade levels. Many upper-grade level teachers have students come to the primary grades to share what they have learned or read to the younger students. Share what (and how) your students have learned with upper-level teachers and challenge them to use your strategies.
- Share the higher-level learning skills that are happening in your classroom by posting signs advertising the value of play centers. Examples of signs can be found on the following Web site: http://www.abcteach.com.

Pulling It All Together

When creating a learning-centered classroom, the teacher

- learns how to speak in terms the rest of the academic community understands;
- shares regularly (daily) about the deep and meaningful work students are doing in the classroom;
- finds ways for caregivers, peers, and the community to learn more about the deep learning in the classroom; and
- finds ways for caregivers, peers, and the community to come into the classroom to see how students are learning.

Reflection . . .

- What do I do to celebrate the learning in my classroom?
- How do I share what is learned in the classroom with the school and the community?
- Do I know how to effectively use technology?
- Whom do I know who can help me learn more about the technology?
- How do I communicate with caregivers, peers, and the community?

Key 10

Form Alliances With Colleagues and Commit to Your Own Professional Development

The teachers who get "burned out" are not *the ones who are constantly learning, which can be exhilarating, but those who feel they must stay in control and ahead of the students at all times.*

—Frank Smith

Learning-Centered Means Everyone, Every Day—No Exceptions

For a kindergarten to be fully learning-centered, the teacher must also be a learner. This is accomplished by establishing a learning culture among kindergarten teachers. Teachers who are learners create and participate in professional learning communities at school, seek mentors, form partnerships with other teachers at their grade level, take advantage of all district-level professional development opportunities, and participate in the learning opportunities of local, regional, state, and national conferences. It is through the learning process that the teacher develops more effective teaching practices, better understands the way children learn, and grows as a professional.

Begin With Collaboration

A high level of commitment and dedication to understanding children and how they learn is essential for teachers of learning-centered classrooms. Educators who set goals for themselves and seek out research or in-service training to better serve the needs of their students are more successful in meeting those needs. Those who research either on their own or with peers produce strategies that will support the child learner. Going from research to practice creates a truly diverse learning community, one where all children (and adults) learn, every day—no exceptions. This learning process allows for teachers to share what works in the way of motivating students, gaining their attention, and increasing their commitment to learn what is being taught, which results in both teachers and students achieving and maintaining a higher level of success.

This approach provides the teacher with an opportunity to know his or her students more deeply, which in turn allows for more opportunities to make choices about how to pursue learning goals. It is imperative that teachers become knowledgeable and skilled observers of children in order to make informed decisions when designing and implementing meaningful and interesting work for their students. Teachers who routinely observe, take anecdotal notes, and document conversations of their students are more effective when they share this information with other teachers and parents or caregivers. For example, Mrs. Worthington is a teacher with ten years' experience in kindergarten. Most considered her the quintessential kindergarten teacher—vivacious, enthusiastic, and a true advocate of children. She spends at least an hour a day "kid watching"—listening, observing interactions, and taking notes. During this time, she not only listens for the developmental progress of her students, but she takes note of their conversations about their home life, interests, and experiences away from school. Once the children are gone, she reviews her notes and uses them to design lessons that would interest her students. When her grade level meets for the weekly meetings, she often shares areas of concern with her colleagues. While she has a great deal of knowledge, it is important for her to hear the input of her peers about the situation. This peer feedback would either confirm what she thought to be true or give her new ideas to try that she had not considered.

By working with their professional peers—having collegial conversations about student needs and how to address them, sharing strategies learned during campus and district training, and brainstorming ideas for lesson design based upon the students' work—teachers take on a leadership role that promotes a learning environment for all. The discussions and interactions with the pedagogical team provide a set of professional tools that benefit both the teacher and learner, as well as give the group more value and a feeling of solidarity. It pushes the teacher to try new strategies and to grow as a professional, a true testament to the learning-centered environment.

It is important to understand that, in the learning-centered classroom, adults and children learn differently. They use different strategies, understand different sets of procedures, and make different assumptions. When adults use themselves as learning models, they must avoid the temptation of allowing the children to simply state what they already know. A true teacher nurtures the sense of amazement and wonder of the world around them. The learning depends upon the child and, as revealed in earlier chapters, much of this is a discovery process for the teacher. While there are standards to be met and the district may have a scope and sequence or planned curriculum, the child will ultimately determine how much time will be needed, what situations are favorable for learning, and what preparations the teacher will need to organize. Through discussions with the learner, the teacher can gain insights into what works. Children are eager to share ideas, make suggestions, ask questions, and solve problems. These offerings paired with the teacher's understanding of learning can produce a powerful and effective learning environment.

Professional Development

As with all things in teaching, the first step comes with knowing the students. The first few weeks of school consist of learning as much as possible about who they are, how they work best, their interests, and what they want to learn about. Kindergarten may be the first formal schooling for some students, so they may not know that they need a quiet place to work or that they work better in the morning than the afternoon. They may also not know all the topics of interest they will want to learn throughout the year. These are things you will discover together as the year progresses—and is part of the fun of teaching kindergarten. Teachers can learn about what their students currently know and what interests them, a little about their family and home culture, and about any physical or learning challenges the student may have. Teachers can start their research by learning more about students on their own. For example, if a student has a learning disability a teacher is unfamiliar with, he or she can research the condition through discussions with the parent or caregiver, school special education teacher, and other district professionals who may have information about the student. The teacher can attend conferences or workshops dealing specifically with that particular condition. This information will provide the teacher with more tools for effectively meeting the needs of that student and, most likely, all the students in the classroom. There are more ideas and strategies listed at the end of this chapter.

Classroom Snapshot—
Ms. Lawrence and Ms. Simmon

At the end of the school year, Ms. Lawrence reviews her teaching performance with her principal and creates a list of things she would like to improve for the following year. One item on her list is to become more comfortable with the use of technology. While she is able to use her e-mail and perform Internet searches, she does not feel she is proficient enough with the technology, something her students are always very interested in doing. Most weeks, the children listen to interactive books or go to Web sites that reinforce skills, but they are never allowed to create an original product on the computer—mainly because of their teacher's uneasiness with this tool. The principal suggests that Ms. Lawrence participate in some summer professional development provided by the district. There are several options and ability levels for her to choose from, and there is an opportunity for her to take part in an action research project to use and reinforce the information gained from the training. She shares this information with a grade-level colleague, Ms. Simmon, who decides to take the summer courses with her.

The weeklong summer training session begins with the very basics of computer use, explaining everything from turning on the computer to using the Internet. As the instructors share information, they allow the teachers to apply what they learned immediately by creating an activity that they could use with their students the following fall. For their first assignment, Ms. Lawrence and Ms. Simmon create an interactive list of Web links their children can use to reinforce skills or to do a simple search for a project. These pre-approved links provide some choice and independence for the young learners without the fear of them accidentally going to inappropriate Web sites. Often teachers are concerned about safeguarding procedures for the students while they are on the Internet. Ms. Lawrence and Ms. Simmon begin planning which links to put on the pages and collaborate which concepts each teacher will research. By the end of the week, the two teachers can create podcasts, video clips, and virtual books.

They are excited and eager for the school year to begin so they can use what they have learned with their students.

The following week, Ms. Lawrence and Ms. Simmon participate in an action research training course. They learn how to collect and interpret data as well as how to share the data with others in the training session. While initially neither teacher was enthusiastic about participating in a research project, by the end of the training they realize how important it is to chart the students' progress and share their successes with their research peers as well as with each other.

During the remaining summer, the two teachers meet to discuss and plan how to use their newly acquired skills in their classroom. They solicit the help of colleagues they know are more computer savvy to brainstorm possible projects for their students in the coming school year. They practice using different software programs to become more familiar with how they work and create templates for an electronic portfolio for their future students' work to be inserted. They work together, knowing that once the school year begins, it will be difficult to incorporate unfamiliar teaching strategies at the last minute.

Soon, the summer is over and the two teachers meet their students. Ms. Lawrence and Ms. Simmon meet at least once a week to discuss their students' needs and ability levels and how they could each do more to integrate technology into their classrooms. Ms. Lawrence starts out slowly. She first uses the computer note card with the Web links for her students to choose from and then moves to more complex projects using video and a movie-editing program. With each successful use of this new tool, she gains professional confidence and personal information about the proficiency level of her students' knowledge of computers. Surprisingly, many of them were very comfortable with navigating on the computer. They are proficient at using the mouse and almost intuitive in their knowledge about how to troubleshoot some technology problems. It occurs to her that this technology is what they know—it isn't new or foreign—it is just another part of their world, just as much as the sun and air and cartoons on Saturday mornings.

Ms. Simmon feels more confident right away. While she too initially uses the Web link page, she realizes sooner how comfortable her students are with the technology and integrates it daily into their academic routine. Soon, her students are able to take digital photographs and create electronic picture books to correlate with the concepts being explored in the classroom. As Ms. Simmon's students are allowed to explore, create, and produce new projects, she shares their progress with Ms. Lawrence. The success of Ms. Simmon's students gives Ms. Lawrence more confidence to try the project herself.

By the end of the year, the two teachers review their research project and realize how the collaboration was just as important as the research itself. They agree that without the support and exchange of ideas, neither teacher would have accomplished as much nor would their students have made so much progress. Each feels that the excitement and enthusiasm of the other helped to keep the momentum going forward.

Reflection on the Classroom Snapshot

In this snapshot, Ms. Lawrence and Ms. Simmon are not only researching topics and information that will benefit their students but each is looking at how her own professional growth impacts the learning of the students. Through collaboration, the teachers are able to create a more exciting and interesting learning experience for everyone—including themselves. Ms. Lawrence discovers that she has had low expectations of her students in the past. Once she allowed the students to use the technology, Ms. Lawrence realized they were not afraid of it but rather eager to use it. She also realized that everyone produced more creative projects when technology was integrated into the curriculum.

Ms. Simmon also learned a great deal about integrating the technology in ways she might never have considered had she not worked with Ms. Lawrence. She found the learning experiences she created and shared with Ms. Lawrence made teaching more interesting for her as well. She enjoyed the challenge of doing something new and exciting with her students and watching them become more successful and independent with each new project.

Strategy: Do the research.

School improvement is most surely and thoroughly achieved when teachers engage in frequent, continuous and increasingly concrete talk about teaching practices . . . [and are] capable of distinguishing one practice and its virtue from another.

—Judith Warren

The word *research* can be an ominous term for educators. Visions of endless tape recording and transcribing, being buried under volumes of heavy books, or being chained to the computer can intimidate teachers who are already overwhelmed with the day-to-day responsibilities of teaching. For Ms. Lawrence, the research was simply a reflection of her performance in areas she felt she needed to improve upon to provide a better learning experience for her students. Ms. Simmon used the research to guide her decisions for instructing her students in the days ahead. While neither teacher is wrong in her view—the research should track and monitor whatever you are trying to improve—for most teachers the view of research would be more aligned with Ms. Simmon's purpose to improve instruction in order to improve student performance.

Research does not need to be an arduous task, but rather it should be a regular part of the teaching day. The purpose of research in this case is to gain information and examine the interests and needs of your students so you can facilitate learning through those interests. If you are doing the research to benefit your students, then make it as simple as possible by documenting casual conversations of the students (with each other and with you). This type of observation can provide a great deal of information for you and a starting point for further investigation.

An excellent example of this is in the book *The Hundred Languages of Children: The Reggio Emilia Approach—Advanced Reflections, Second Edition,* by Edwards, Gandini, and Forman (1998). The book compares the teaching practices of early childhood teachers in the Reggio area of Italy with teaching practices here in the United States. The example in the book involves a dinosaur project created through the interests of a group of students in the class. The teacher finds that there are eight children who seem to have a deep interest in dinosaurs. She discovers this fact through casual conversations, items brought to school, and so forth. Since the entire class will not be participating in the project, the group of eight students begins by sitting at a table, drawing dinosaurs and discussing what they know. (It is the philosophy of this approach that deeper, more intense learning occurs when the student is truly interested in the project and that the whole group benefits when the students share what they have learned with them.)

From the initial session, the students then work with the teacher to create a list of questions that they are interested in learning more about. The teacher then collaborates with other teachers and a curriculum specialist to brainstorm possible directions the learning experiences can go through this project as well as formulating "provocative questions" to gain more information about the depth of knowledge the students have about dinosaurs.

Throughout the next several weeks, the students move through a problem solving process that evolves from deciding upon what problems to investigate (the time the dinosaurs lived, size and dimensions of dinosaurs, how dinosaurs died), and where to find the information to solve their problems, to creating 3-D models and life-sized representations of dinosaurs to display in the school. The teacher records conversations to review and later provides a variety of materials to help move the process forward. She does not provide quick answers to their questions, but rather she allows them the opportunity and time to come to their own conclusions.

The students' progress and direct quotes are displayed for the entire school to view, acknowledging and valuing their contributions to the learning community. This display provides documentation of the learning process as well as providing a learning opportunity for others not involved in the project. This affirmation of what the students know and have learned motivates them to continue learning, even when the learning is challenging.

So how does the Reggio approach apply to the school system here in the States? In many ways, the philosophies of the two countries are very similar. Most teachers of young children believe that each child has his or her own developmental time clock; however, the imposing of state standards has complicated the teaching process by confusing some teachers who now believe the state curriculum takes precedence over developmental practice. In the example from the scenario above, deep and profound learning occurred within the domains of developmentally appropriate practice. Much of what is learned by the children during the dinosaur project would exceed many of our state standards, but because the students were intensely interested in the topic and desired to know more, they were motivated to proceed, even though the journey was very challenging.

Pulling It All Together

When creating a learning-centered classroom, the teacher

- is consistently and constantly learning about his or her students and about the content to grow as a professional;
- deeply knows the students and what they are interested in learning more about;
- researches topics and information to better facilitate learning for the students;
- seeks out professional development opportunities in order to grow;
- works collegially to develop ideas and strategies to better assist in the learning process;
- provides opportunities for students to learn and participate in projects of interest;
- values the comments and work of peers, regularly seeking out their professional opinions and judgments; and
- regularly seeks out mentors or peers with whom to collaborate, create, grow professionally, and team teach.

Reflection . . .

- How do I show my students that I value learning?
- Do I know enough about my students to provide meaningful work for them?
- Do I provide opportunities for them to problem solve deeply?
- Do I give students the answers or allow them to discover the answers?
- How do I change my teaching to better align with the way my students learn?
- Do I do the same activities year after year or tailor them to meet the needs of my students?
- In what areas do I need to grow as a professional?
- How do I collaborate with others?
- What can I learn from others?
- Is there someone I know whom I could work with regularly to plan and grow professionally?

Resources

Key One Resources

Scent Jars

Fill film containers with cotton balls dipped in essential oils (easily found at hobby or craft stores). Picture cards (made using clip art) that match the scents create a fun way to assess what the children have learned. Label the bottom of the scent jars (or use colored dots) to create a matching game that is self-assessing for the students.

Scented Play Dough Recipe

1 cup all-purpose flour   1 tablespoon vegetable oil
½ cup salt   2 teaspoons cream of tartar
1 cup water   food coloring
1 teaspoon essential oils or food extract

Combine all ingredients except food coloring and extract. Cook and stir over medium heat until mixture forms a ball (approximately 3 minutes). Remove from heat. Divide and add food coloring and essential oils or extract to each portion. Knead several minutes on wax paper until dough is smooth and workable. (This will be very warm—handle carefully.)

Writing Prompt

The student creates a journal page using a pre-assigned prompt. This activity grows with the students' ability. The teacher provides dictation for those who need the help. As phonemic awareness and literacy development progress, the student will be able to write his or her own response.

Today I learned about _____.

Procedures for Successful Centers
(See the Centers Checklist that follows.)

- Students use the Centers Checklist to document which learning centers they have completed. The learning centers can be repeated for a number of days. The students fill in the smiley faces as they complete the centers. Revisiting a center during the week provides a student with more practice and the opportunity to master and move forward toward more complex skill development. This also allows students who need more time to complete tasks that are difficult an opportunity to experience all centers at least once during the week. The teacher is also given an opportunity to observe and document children interacting in a variety of learning situations. Providing a picture from clip art gives the child a visual to allow them an element of independence.
- Color code each learning center so the students can organize their day. The teacher can direct students to choose at least one center of each color per day. If language arts centers are all the same color, they will be sure to have a more balanced academic day.
- Limit the number of students at each learning center to no more than four for better management of supplies and procedures.

Student_____ Date:_____

Center	Completed
Lang. Arts: Journal Writing	☺ ☺ ☺ ☺ ☺
Lang. Arts: Listening Center– Very Hungry Caterpillar	☺ ☺ ☺ ☺ ☺
Science: Fruit Compare	☺ ☺ ☺ ☺ ☺
Dramatic Play: Social St. Grocery Store	☺ ☺ ☺ ☺ ☺
Block Center	☺ ☺ ☺ ☺ ☺
Math: Patterning – Fruit Kabobs	☺ ☺ ☺ ☺ ☺
Math: Graphing Fruit Shapes	☺ ☺ ☺ ☺ ☺
Art: Scented Paint Pictures	☺ ☺ ☺ ☺ ☺
Fine Motor: Scented Play Dough	☺ ☺ ☺ ☺ ☺
Sand Table	☺ ☺ ☺ ☺ ☺
Computers	☺ ☺ ☺ ☺ ☺

Student_____ Date:_____

Center	Completed
Lang. Arts: Journal Writing	☺ ☺ ☺ ☺ ☺
Lang. Arts: Listening Center– Very Hungry Caterpillar	☺ ☺ ☺ ☺ ☺
Science: Fruit Compare	☺ ☺ ☺ ☺ ☺
Dramatic Play: Social St. Grocery Store	☺ ☺ ☺ ☺ ☺
Block Center	☺ ☺ ☺ ☺ ☺
Math: Patterning – Fruit Kabobs	☺ ☺ ☺ ☺ ☺
Math: Graphing Fruit Shapes	☺ ☺ ☺ ☺ ☺
Art: Scented Paint Pictures	☺ ☺ ☺ ☺ ☺
Fine Motor: Scented Play Dough	☺ ☺ ☺ ☺ ☺
Sand Table	☺ ☺ ☺ ☺ ☺
Computers	☺ ☺ ☺ ☺ ☺

Key Two Resources

Week of:

Assessments

Student	Center 1: Math M&M Graphing	Center 2: Language Arts Journals	Center 3: Science Recording sink/float	Center 4: Social Studies Comparing stamps from around the world	Center 5: Computers Starfall.com—short *a*
Angelina	divides candy into groups by color and correctly records colors on graph	writes about weekend — dad coming home from Iraq. Wonderfully detailed picture and inverted spelling			successfully matches short *a* picture words
Anthony		writes about weekend trip — no attempt at writing, draws simple pictures — people do not have arms	correctly recorded all 10 sink/float findings using simple pictures		
Cathy	successful in sorting, counting, and recording on graph		correctly recorded all 10 sink/float findings	records comparisons — draws pictures of stamp colors	
Deangelo	sorts and counts candies correctly, but exhibits some difficulty in representing on graph	Writes about weekend — family plays video games. Attempts to write words, complex and detailed picture			successfully matches short *a* picture words
Marcus			correctly recorded all 10 sink/float findings	records comparisons — sorts stamps by size	successfully matches short *a* picture words

142

Week of:

Assessments

Student	Center 1:	Center 2:	Center 3:	Center 4:	Center 5:

Dear Families,

This year our class will participate in a yearlong investigation of the world around us. We will explore all the natural and cultural wonders around us with many excursions into the neighborhood and surrounding community. We will also investigate the world beyond our boundaries through a fun character by the name of Flat Stanley. Flat Stanley is a character from a book written by Jeff Brown. According to the story, Flat Stanley is accidentally flattened by a bulletin board in his sleep. While this sounds tragic and scary to us, it allows this young man to have many adventures as he is able to be sent in the mail all over the world.

Our class would like to send Flat Stanley on more adventures, but we need your help! Please take a few minutes to think of five people your child could send Flat Stanley to. In order to have a variety of places to study, try to think of people who may be in different states or countries. Please contact these people to let them know that Flat Stanley will be coming with an instruction letter. Flat Stanley will be asking to stay with the host for a short visit to see the sites and points of interest of that area and perhaps collect pictures, brochures, postcards, or souvenirs. Once Stanley's visit is over, the host will mail him back to you. We will mail Stanley to each of the five people on your list.

We are eager to begin this project and to learn more about the world around us! Thanks in advance for helping us with this exciting learning opportunity. If you have questions, please contact me at school.

Sincerely,

Key Three Resources

A. Attention-Deficit/Hyperactivity Disorder

Inattention: The student may exhibit a combination of the following:	Things to Try	Hyperactivity: The student may exhibit a combination of the following:	Things to Try	Impulsivity: The student may exhibit a combination of the following:	Things to Try
Often makes careless mistakes in schoolwork or other activities.	Assign a buddy to help student remember the steps or directions.	Fidgets with hands or feet or squirms in seat.	Provide sensory breaks, squishy balls, pieces of fur, etc. as well as ample opportunities for gross motor activities.	Blurts out answers before questions have been finished.	Frequent pre-minders of expectations.
Does not pay close attention to details and may not follow directions.	Give only one- or two-step directions—wait until student has completed before giving next direction.	Often gets up from seat when remaining in seat is expected.	Investigate the use of a sensory or sponge seat for the child. Lower the table so a chair is not necessary. The child sits on floor and/or cushion and is literally grounded.	Has a problem waiting one's turn. Often interrupts or intrudes on others.	Create a signal for student to remind him or her not to interrupt.
Does not seem to be listening when spoken to directly—even when name is spoken.	Be sure to gain eye contact with student when giving directions. Have student repeat directions before allowing them to begin.	Often runs around and/or climbs when and where it is not appropriate.	Provide an adult buddy to hold hand of student during these times. This is a safety issue—not a punishment for the child.		
Disorganized with materials, use of time and activities.	Provide a special container or area for materials. Use visuals for time allotments, use timers.	Has difficulty playing or enjoying leisure activities quietly.	Find topics of interest that can be translated into relaxing activities—books, puzzles, collections of high interest topics.		
Avoids things that take a lot of mental concentration for an extended period of time.	Provide frequent breaks—allow student to move from a difficult activity to an easier or more enjoyable activity. Break difficult activity into smaller increments.	Is often on the go or often acts as if driven by a motor.	Provide activities that focus the energy productively.		
Easily distracted—has trouble paying attention to tasks or play activities.	Use headphones or earmuffs to create a barrier to outside stimuli.	Talks excessively.	Allow many opportunities for conversations with peers, in front of the whole group, and with adults on a variety of topics.		
Forgetful in daily activities.	Provide a picture chart of daily routine.				

From *Diagnostic and Statistical Manual of Mental Disorders* (4th Edition), 2000, Washington, D.C.: American Psychiatric Association. © 2000 by American Psychiatric Association. Adapted with permission.

B. Autism Spectrum Disorders

Social Interactions: The student may exhibit a combination of the following:	Things to Try	Communication Skills: The student may exhibit a combination of the following:	Things to Try	Patterns of Behavior, Interests, and Activities: The student may exhibit a combination of the following:	Things to Try
May resist eye contact, lack of facial expression, body posture, and gestures to regulate social interaction.	Physical therapy, music and movement activities.	A delay or total lack of spoken language. Does not attempt to compensate through alternative modes of communication such as gestures.	Provide opportunities to communicate with others, paying attention to facial expressions, tone, pitch and cadence, as well as body language.	Preoccupation with one or more patterns of interest, such as watching a spinning top or moving parts of a toy.	Provide opportunities for the child to interact with others and a variety of other objects.
Prefers playing and working alone, retreats into a private world.	Alternate easy or desired activities with more difficult ones, provide options for working with others.	Individuals with adequate speech may have marked impairment in ability to keep a conversation going.	Communication or speech therapy may be necessary.	Inflexible adherence to specific, nonfunctional routines, schedules, or rituals.	Keep schedules as normal as possible. Share any changes of schedules with child before they happen.
Unable to share enjoyment, interests, or achievements with other people.	Use art activities to allow the child an opportunity to express feelings.	May use repetitive language or create a personal language mode, such as a singsong or robot-like voice or using irregular rhythm.	Music provides a safe and structured way to communicate.	Transitions cause emotional stress.	Provide picture cue cards to indicate schedule and remind child what event is coming next.
Unaware of how others feel or how actions affect others.	Use music in the classroom to provide immediate feedback and tap into emotions.	Lack of ability to participate in spontaneous make-believe or dramatic play appropriate to development level.	Provide opportunities for supervised dramatic play interaction with others.	Performs repetitive motor mannerisms such as rubbing hands, flapping arms, rocking, pacing, or spinning body.	Music and movement activities that provide an outlet for repetitive movements and vocal patterns.
				May be hypersensitive to light, sound, or touch.	Provide frequent sensory breaks—if noise is too stimulating, provide quiet space.

From *Diagnostic and Statistical Manual of Mental Disorders* (4th Edition), 1994, Washington, D.C.: American Psychiatric Association. © 1994 by American Psychiatric Association. And National Autism Association. Retrieved Oct. 15, 2007, from http://www.nationalautismassociation.org. Adapted with Permission.

Key Five Resources

Glyphs

What is a glyph? A glyph is a creative way for students to collect, display, and interpret data. Students create pictures in which each part of the picture represents a unique bit of personal data about themselves. Once the picture is completed, it can be used to compare each attribute with the other students in the class.

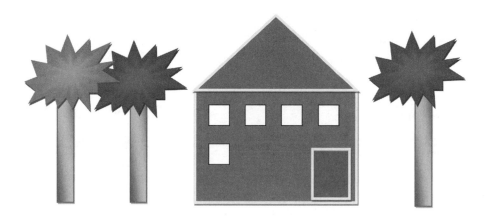

1. Make a house using the square tool. Fill the square with your favorite color.

2. Make the roof using the triangle tool. Fill the triangle with red if you are a girl and orange if you are a boy.

3. Using the square tool, make the number of windows on your house equal your age.

4. Using the square tool, add a door to your house. Make the house yellow if you like chocolate ice cream best or purple if you like vanilla best.

5. Make a tree using the rectangle tool for the trunk and the star tool for the treetop. Make as many trees as you have brothers and sisters. Make the treetops green for each brother. Make the treetops red for each sister.

The example above was created using a drawing program. The teacher reads the first direction, being sure to wait until all students have completed it before going on to the next (if doing a whole class project). Depending on how much computer lab time your class is alloted, this may take more than one class period. If the teacher decides to do this individually on classroom computers, he or she may want each child to complete only the first direction and then move on—or the teacher may sit with each child at the computer to give individual directions. When all glyphs are completed, each direction is a different graphing opportunity: for example, (1) Classmates' Favorite Colors. (2) How Many Boys and Girls Are in Class? (3) How Old Are We? (4) What Do We Like Best, Chocolate or Vanilla? (5) How Many Siblings Do We Have?

Reading Arbor
Materials needed
2 one-inch dowels (each approx. 5 feet long)
4 eye fasteners
chain
plastic plant hooks
20 feet of floral or other decorative garland

Directions

1. Screw one eye hook into each end of the dowels.

2. Attach chain to eye hooks.

3. Slide hooks onto support rods of ceiling.

4. Hang dowels from hooks by the chain as far apart as you want the arbor to be.

5. Create the arbor by wrapping decorative garland from one dowel to the next.

Key Six Resources

Daily Newsletters

This is a common practice among kindergarten teachers. It allows students to learn about their classmates, thus creating a learning community, and it provides rich literacy learning opportunities, including print awareness, sentence structure, and phonemic awareness.

Mrs. Macrone's Class News

Today is Thursday, October 18, 2007. The weather is warm and sunny.

Today we will learn about fire safety. A fire truck will come to our school.

Yesterday Kim's dad came home from Iraq. She is very happy.

Tomorrow will be Jason's birthday. His mom will bring cupcakes. We will sing *Happy Birthday* to him.

Today Sam and Noah are absent.

Superstar Student

Giving a student a time to shine as well as providing opportunities to build a caring classroom community is always a good idea. The letter below is an example of how to get started. Providing an area for the students to decorate with items about themselves is also encouraged. Be sure that valuable or tempting items are not left in the Superstar Student display area overnight or take special care to ensure the items are returned.

I Am a Superstar Student!

1. My favorite foods are:

_____

2. Things I like to do:

_____

3. My family is special because :

_____

4. Someday I would like to:

_____

5. Something you should know about me:

_____

Dear Family,

Next week, March 22–26, your child is the classroom SUPER-STAR! We want to celebrate your child's uniqueness! Please help your child fill out the attached form. If you have pictures or other items that your child could share with us, please send them Monday, March 22 with the form so we can create your child's SUPERSTAR display.

Thanks for allowing us to celebrate your child.

Family Newsletters

To create a learning environment that respects and values the family home culture, letters going home should be in the home language. If you are not bilingual and need assistance, ask caregivers or colleagues to assist. Teachers should also remember that just because someone speaks another language does not mean that person also reads the language. There are many language translation programs on the Internet, but be aware that the literal translation of information often is not correct when translated into cultural dialects and speaking patterns. Before you send home any written communication, ask caregivers to indicate which language they are most comfortable using when communicating.

Kindergarten News

This week we are learning about all things TEXAS! We will be studying the following state symbols:

- flower—blue bonnet
- tree—pecan
- large mammal—longhorn
- small mammal—armadillo
- capital—Austin
- food—chili

We will be sending home a book with these Texas symbols for your child to share with you. Please take a few minutes to share this book with your child.

March Birthdays!!
Some of our friends will be turning 6 years old!

Happy Birthday to:

Juan—14th
Sarah—22nd

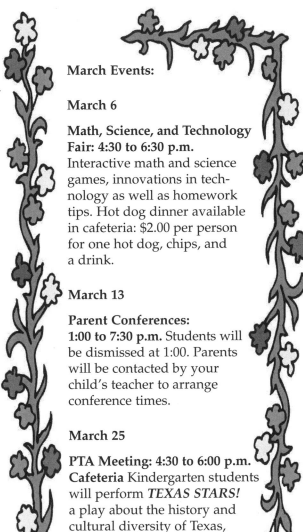

March Events:

March 6

Math, Science, and Technology Fair: 4:30 to 6:30 p.m. Interactive math and science games, innovations in technology as well as homework tips. Hot dog dinner available in cafeteria: $2.00 per person for one hot dog, chips, and a drink.

March 13

Parent Conferences: 1:00 to 7:30 p.m. Students will be dismissed at 1:00. Parents will be contacted by your child's teacher to arrange conference times.

March 25

PTA Meeting: 4:30 to 6:00 p.m. Cafeteria Kindergarten students will perform *TEXAS STARS!* a play about the history and cultural diversity of Texas, starring your child!!

Noticias del Kindergarten

Esta semana estamos aprendiendo sobre todas las cosas TEXAS!! Estudiaremos los símbolos siguientes del estado:

- capo del azul de la flor
- árbol—nueces
- mamífero grande—fonolocalizador de vacas
- mamífero pequeño—armadillo
- capital—Austin
- alimento—chili

Enviaremos hogar un libro con estos símbolos de Tejas para que su niño comparta con usted. Tome por favor algunos minutos para compartir este libro con su niño.

¡Cumpleaños de marzo!!
Feliz cumpleaños nuestros amigitos:

Juan—14th
Sarah—22nd

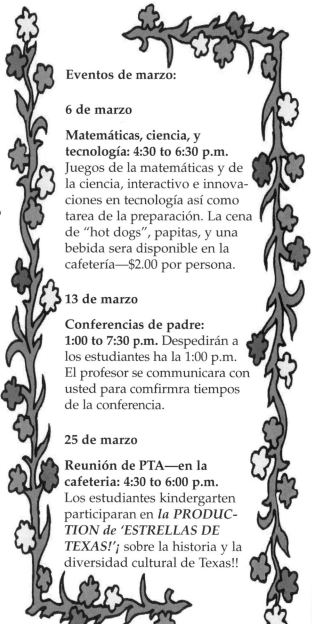

Eventos de marzo:

6 de marzo

Matemáticas, ciencia, y tecnología: 4:30 to 6:30 p.m. Juegos de la matemáticas y de la ciencia, interactivo e innovaciones en tecnología así como tarea de la preparación. La cena de "hot dogs", papitas, y una bebida sera disponible en la cafetería—$2.00 por persona.

13 de marzo

Conferencias de padre: 1:00 to 7:30 p.m. Despedirán a los estudiantes ha la 1:00 p.m. El profesor se communicara con usted para comfirmra tiempos de la conferencia.

25 de marzo

Reunión de PTA—en la cafeteria: 4:30 to 6:00 p.m. Los estudiantes kindergarten participaran en *la PRODUCTION de 'ESTRELLAS DE TEXAS!'¡* sobre la historia y la diversidad cultural de Texas!!

Key Eight Resources

Parent Caregiver Surveys

Finding out as much as you can about your students and their families can be an easy process through simple surveys. Examples of two surveys are shown below. Gaining information from caregivers to include and embrace the family culture can also be accomplished by sending home weekly journals and simply asking caregivers to provide input about topics to be covered in the classroom.

Dear Families,

Welcome to Kindergarten! This year your child will learn many new things—letter recognition, number concepts—and will be exploring the world through science and social studies as well as learning about and respecting the similarities and differences of all people. You are an important element in this process, and I need your help.

You are your child's most important teacher. As a teacher, you know best how your child learns, his/her interests, and what motivates your child to continue working even when the task is difficult. Please take a few minutes to fill out the survey below so that I can better understand your child and can design learning experiences that will better serve your child's needs.

You are part of the learning community, so please share with me any information you feel will benefit your child's learning experience. As a team, we will continue to work together throughout the year and ensure your child has a wonderful learning experience in kindergarten this year.

Thank you in advance for your cooperation and participation!

Caregiver Survey

1. Please list at least five topics of interest your child enjoys. (Rocks, dinosaurs, etc.)

   _____
   _____
   _____
   _____

2. Please list activities your child likes to do at home. (Listening to stories, playing games, video games, etc.)

   _____
   _____
   _____
   _____

3. How does your child learn best? (Hands-on experiences, watching and then trying it, listening to directions and then doing it, or other ways)

   _____
   _____
   _____
   _____

4. Please list any areas of concern you may have about your child.

   _____
   _____
   _____
   _____

5. Please list any other information I need to know about your child.

   _____
   _____
   _____
   _____

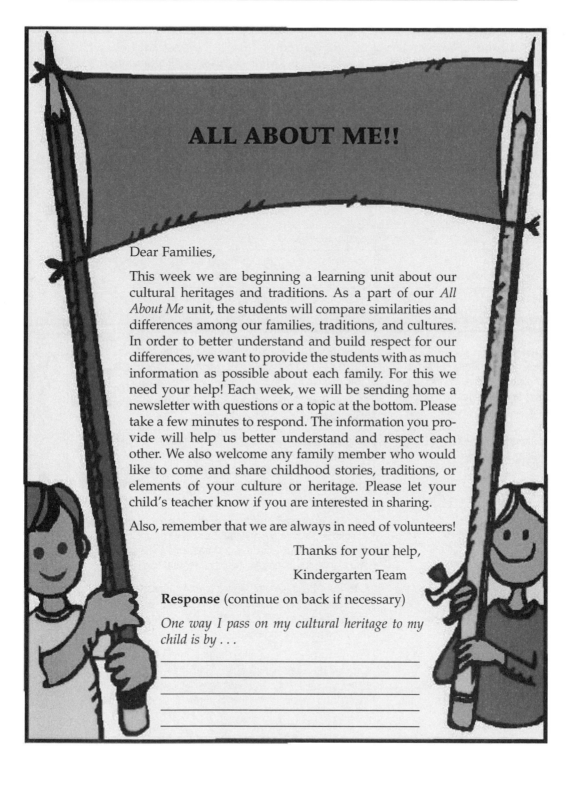

ALL ABOUT ME!!

Dear Families,

This week we are beginning a learning unit about our cultural heritages and traditions. As a part of our *All About Me* unit, the students will compare similarities and differences among our families, traditions, and cultures. In order to better understand and build respect for our differences, we want to provide the students with as much information as possible about each family. For this we need your help! Each week, we will be sending home a newsletter with questions or a topic at the bottom. Please take a few minutes to respond. The information you provide will help us better understand and respect each other. We also welcome any family member who would like to come and share childhood stories, traditions, or elements of your culture or heritage. Please let your child's teacher know if you are interested in sharing.

Also, remember that we are always in need of volunteers!

Thanks for your help,

Kindergarten Team

Response (continue on back if necessary)

One way I pass on my cultural heritage to my child is by . . .

_____

_____

_____

_____

_____

Identify Flowers Lesson Plan

Identify Flowers lesson is adapted from *Beyond Heroes and Holidays: A Practical Guide to K–12 Anti-Racist, Multicultural Education and Staff Development.* The individual lesson plan template follows the lesson for times when you may be appraised and need to turn in a single lesson plan to an administrator.

Identity Flowers Lesson Plan	
Teacher Name	
Grade Level	
Subject/Unit	
Lesson Title	Identity Flowers
Brief Description *What do the students do in this lesson?*	Students make construction paper flowers; each petal is decorated to represent an aspect of their identity.
Big Ideas *What central ideas or fundamental principles are the focus of this lesson?*	People are similar in some ways and different in others. Both the similarities and the differences should be acknowledged, respected, and embraced in a community.
Objectives *What specific knowledge or skills do you want the students to learn, practice, or experience as a result of participation in this lesson?*	Students will identify aspects of their identity that are important to them (race, culture, languages spoken, family structure, etc.) Students will see their similarities and differences with their classmates.
State Standards/Pre-K Guidelines Addressed	State Standards—Social Studies K.11 The student understands similarities and differences among people. The student is expected to: (A) identify personal attributes common to all people such as physical characteristics; (B) identify differences among people. K.12 The student understands how people learn about themselves through family customs and traditions. The student is expected to: (A) identify family customs and traditions and explain their importance; (B) compare family customs and traditions. K.16 The student communicates in oral and visual forms. The student is expected to: (A) express ideas orally based on knowledge and experiences; (B) create and interpret visuals including pictures and maps. PRE-K GUIDELINES—Social Studies: Individual, Culture, and Community. The child identifies similarities among people like himself/herself and classmates as well as among himself/herself and people from other cultures.

Materials Needed	An artificial or real flower
List all of the materials needed to teach this lesson. Be as detailed as possible. (Include any additional materials needed for differentiated instruction accommodations listed below.)	Construction paper of assorted colors Markers Scissors Glue sticks Space on bulletin board to display finished work Stapler and staples for hanging finished work
Preparation and Set-up	This lesson requires two 30-minute blocks of time.
Describe how the materials should be prepared, set up, and organized. Be as detailed as possible.	Prep for Part One: Construction paper, markers, scissors, and glue sticks are set on each table
	Prep for Part Two: Mount all of the children's flowers on a bulletin board labeled "We are beautiful flowers." Have a stepstool handy for children to be able to see the flowers that are mounted high on the board.

Procedure

Describe exactly what the teacher and the students do in the lesson. Be specific.

PART ONE

1. Read the class an age-appropriate book about self-identity.
2. Share aspects of your identity with the class; ask volunteers to share aspects of their identities. Keep the conversation focused on substantive issues like race, ethnicity, and language and avoid superficial issues like hair color and favorite foods.
3. Show the students the flower. Make sure that everyone knows the word *petal*. Emphasize the beauty of the flower.
4. Explain that each of us is like a flower—all these different aspects of our identities are like the petals on a flower and it's the unique combination of the petals that makes our flowers beautiful.
5. Introduce activity. The student will cut a circle out of construction paper and write his or her name in the center. The student will cut five flower petals out of construction paper. The student will write or draw one aspect of his or her identity on each petal. The student will glue the petals to the circle in the shape of a flower. The students will bring their finished flowers to the prepared bulletin board to be hung up.
6. Dismiss the students to their tables. Circulate and assist as needed.
7. Mount the students' flowers.

PART TWO

1. Bring the students together in front of the bulletin board. Give each student the opportunity to talk about his or her flower, focusing on the characteristics on each petal.
2. Ask the class to identify similarities and differences between the presenting child and other children who have shared their flowers.
3. Continue until each child has presented.
4. Reread the book used in Part One of the lesson, help children achieve closure.

Evaluation	Work Samples: The completed flowers will show the students' awareness of the concept of identity and of the parts of their identity that are important to them; the students' presentation of their flower to the class will also demonstrate mastery of this concept.
How will you know that students met the lesson objectives?	Class Discussion: Conversations about similarities and differences among the flowers will provide evidence of students' understanding of this concept

(Continued)

Identity Flowers Lesson Plan (Continued)	
Differentiation Plans *How will you modify the lesson to meet the needs of students working above and below grade level?* *How will you make sure these students connect with the lesson's Big Ideas in a meaningful, appropriate way?*	
Objectives: Students grade level *How will you modify the lesson's objectives to meet the needs of students working above grade level?*	
Procedures: Students above grade level *How will you modify the lesson's procedures to meet the needs of students working above grade level?*	
Evaluation: Students above grade level *How will you know that above-level students met their modified objectives?*	
Objectives: Students below grade level *How will you modify the lesson's objectives to meet the needs of students working below grade level?*	
Procedures: Students below grade level *How will you modify the lesson's procedures to meet the needs of students working below grade level?*	
Evaluation: Students below grade level *How will you know that below-level students met their modified objectives?*	

SOURCE: Identify Flowers Lesson Plan by Lisa Goldstein

For a weekly lesson plan format, the following template could work.

Weekly Lesson Plan						
Teacher Name				**Date**		
Math Objectives			**Language Objectives**			
Standards:			**Standards:**			
	Table Games **8:00–8:15**	**Calendar** **8:15–8:30**	**Gross Motor** **8:30–8:45**	**Shared Reading** **8:45–9:00**	**Language/Unit Workshop** **9:00–10:00**	
Monday	TLW: Act: Mat: Ass:	TLW: Act: Mat: Ass:	TLW: Act: Mat: Ass:	Rhyme: Act: Mat: Ass:	TLW: Act: Mat: Ass:	Snack/Restroom 10:00–10:15 / Specials 10:25–11:10
Tuesday	TLW: Act: Mat: Ass:	TLW: Act: Mat: Ass:	TLW: Act: Mat: Ass:	Story: Act: Mat: Ass:	TLW: Act: Mat: Ass:	Snack/Restroom 10:00–10:15 / Specials 10:25–11:10
Wednesday	TLW: Act: Mat: Ass:	TLW: Act: Mat: Ass:	TLW: Act: Mat: Ass:	Story: Act: Mat: Ass:	TLW: Act: Mat: Ass:	Snack/Restroom 10:00–10:15 / Specials 10:25–11:10
Thursday	TLW: Act: Mat: Ass:	TLW: Act: Mat: Ass:	TLW: Act: Mat: Ass:	Story: Act: Mat: Ass:	TLW: Act: Mat: Ass:	Snack/Restroom 10:00–10:15 / Specials 10:25–11:10
Friday	TLW: Act: Mat: Ass:	TLW: Act: Mat: Ass:	TLW: Act: Mat: Ass:	TLW: Act: Mat: Ass:	TLW: Act: Mat: Ass:	Snack/Restroom 10:00–10:15 / Specials 10:25–11:10

(Continued)

Weekly Lesson Plan (Continued)					
Social Studies Objectives			**Science Objectives**		**Physical Development/Technology**
Standards:			**Standards:**		**PD Standards:** **Tech Standards:**
	Read Aloud **11:15–11:40**			**Math Workshop** **1:30–2:00**	**Plan/Do/Review** **2:00–3:00**	**Differentiated** **Instruction**
Monday	Story: Comprehension strategy:	Lunch/Outside 11:48–12:30	Rest 12:30–1:30	TLW: Act: Mat: Ass:	TLW: Act: Mat: Ass: Student activities	
Tuesday	Story: Comprehension strategy:	Lunch/Outside 11:48–12:30	Rest 12:30–1:30	TLW: Act: Mat: Ass:	TLW: Act: Mat: Ass: Student activities	
Wednesday	Story: Comprehension strategy:	Lunch/Outside 11:48–12:30	Rest 12:30–1:30	TLW: Act: Mat: Ass:	TLW: Act: Mat: Ass: Student activities	
Thursday	Story: Comprehension strategy:	Lunch/Outside 11:48–12:30	Rest 12:30–1:30	TLW: Act: Mat: Ass:	TLW:	
Friday	Story: Comprehension strategy:	Lunch/Outside 11:48–12:30	Rest 12:30–1:30	TLW: Act: Mat: Ass:	Act:	

SOURCE: Weekly Lesson plan by Linda C. Wood

Key Nine Resources

Technology in the Classroom

By creating a Web page, teachers can share ideas with other teachers and with the local community about what is being learned in the classroom. The examples below show how a simple Web page can be; there are many free and easy-to-use Web page hosting sites specifically created for teachers. While these examples contain a teacher resource site that shares ideas for integrating technology into the state curriculum, other ideas might be just to create a blogging page or even just to post events on your school's Web page.

WELCOME
to

The TEKnology Web Page

	Kindergarten	First Grade	Second Grade	
Third Grade	Fourth Grade	Fifth Grade	Student Samples	Educational Technology Links

Have a lesson plan idea or question? E-mail us!

Sign Guestbook View Guestbook

Lori Burch, Campus Instructional Technologist
Shari Ehly, Campus Instructional Specialist
Killeen Independent School District, Killeen, Texas

http://www.geocities.com/teknologyprogram/

SOURCE: Welcome to The TEKnology We Page by Lori Burch

Kindergarten TEKS (Texas Essential Knowledge and Skills) Activities

Number, operation, and quantitative reasoning. The concept of number is critical in ordering, labeling, and expressing quantities and relationships. Students describe how they use numbers to solve problems in meaningful contexts and applications and translate informal language into mathematical symbols

Standard K.1A The student uses numbers to name quantities. The student is expected to use one-to-one correspondence and language such as more than, same number as, or two less than to describe relative sizes of sets of concrete objects.

Supporting Software:

1. Muppet Math (Gonzo's Classroom)

2. Muppets on Stage (counting number of objects)

3. Kid Works 2 or KidPix Deluxe: Student could make and label sets (less than, more than, same as) using the stamps and typing tools.

Standard K.1B The student uses numbers to name quantities. The student is expected to use sets of concrete objects to represent quantities given in verbal or written form (through 9).

Supporting Software:

1. Muppet Math

2. Muppets on Stage (number of sets of objects)

3. Kid Works 2 or KidPix Deluxe: Student makes number cards using stamps and typing tools. When finished the teacher could print, laminate, and cut them out for the child to use in center activities.

Standard K.1C The student uses numbers to name quantities. The student is expected to use numbers to describe how many objects are in a set (through 20).

Supporting Software:

1. Muppet Math (Miss Piggy's PE class)

2. Kid Works 2 or KidPix Deluxe: Students create a counting book using stamps and typing tools to record counting situations

from classroom experiences. The teacher can print and use as a portfolio assessment.

Standard K.2A The student describes order of events or objects. The student is expected to use language such as before or after to describe relative position in a sequence of events or objects.

Supporting Software:

1. Snapdragon: The student can move objects to place in order. When working with a partner, they can verbally discuss which objects they found "before" or "after" another.

Allowing students to create electronic products:

Jamie had 9 fish.
He had 8 pieces of food.
Jamie had more fish
than food.

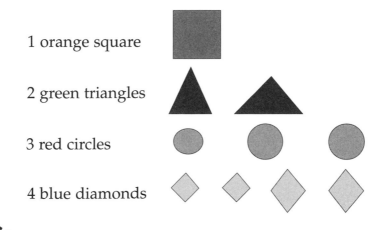

1 orange square

2 green triangles

3 red circles

4 blue diamonds

Communication

The following form can be used as a sign to describe the learning opportunities provided and accomplished by the work displayed on the bulletin board. When the description is dictated by a student, this becomes a powerful message to the school learning community and to families. The state standards should also be listed by the teacher.

Graceland Elementary School

The students created _____ because we are
learning about _____.

This is important work because the state standards require us to learn

_____.

This is an important foundation for learning about _____

_____.

Some vocabulary we learned during this topic of study includes:

_____.

Ask us about this!

Description by: _____
Teacher: _____

Key Ten Resources

Creating a Safe Site Link Page

In the Classroom Snapshot for Key 10, Ms. Lawrence and Ms. Simmon created a safe site linking page. This is an example of such a page. Teachers can create a safe Web site link page by copying the link in the address bar and pasting it into a document table. To help the children identify the link you want them to work in, add icons or clip art pictures.

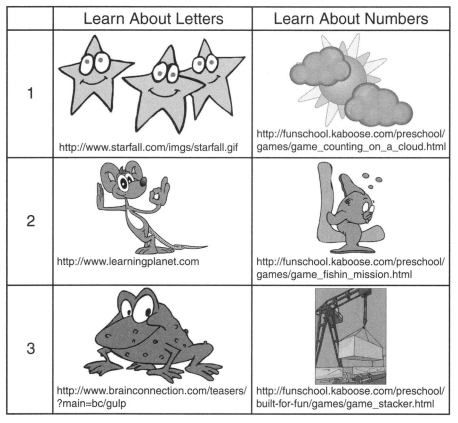

	Learn About Letters	Learn About Numbers
1	http://www.starfall.com/imgs/starfall.gif	http://funschool.kaboose.com/preschool/games/game_counting_on_a_cloud.html
2	http://www.learningplanet.com	http://funschool.kaboose.com/preschool/games/game_fishin_mission.html
3	http://www.brainconnection.com/teasers/?main=bc/gulp	http://funschool.kaboose.com/preschool/built-for-fun/games/game_stacker.html

Clip art found at: http://www.clipart.com

Things to Ask . . .

If you are a novice teacher or a teacher with a recurring issue in your classroom, here are a few questions to ask a trusted colleague—one whose practices match with your belief system about teaching.

Things to Ask Yourself

1. **What is the problem?** Write this down as clearly as you can. It is important to know what it is that you need to work on before you can find a solution. If you have multiple issues, list them in order of priority.

   _____
   _____
   _____

2. **Is the problem academic?** Are students not performing at expected levels? Am I unable to find the gap or learning difficulty preventing a child from meeting benchmarks? Is the child far advanced to classmates, and I am having difficulty finding ways to challenge him or her?

   _____
   _____
   _____

3. **Is the problem related to behavior management strategies?** Are there children who are often off-task? What is the motivation behind the misbehavior? Is there an issue with room or seating arrangement? Are the materials or activities covered too easy or too difficult? Are the students interested and motivated to complete the learning activities?

   _____
   _____
   _____

4. **Is the problem related to making a connection between the standards and developmentally-appropriate practices?** Do I fully understand the standards and what they are asking the students to learn? Who can I ask if I do not know? Do I know what it looks like when the student has mastered the skill or concept taught? What will I do if the student does not master the skill or concept? Is what I feel the students need to learn aligned with what the state standards is asking the children to learn? Do I feel confident in teaching the content I am expected to teach?

   _____
   _____
   _____

5. **How well do I know my students?** What would each child value in the lesson to motivate him or her to complete the assignment? How well do they work with others? Do I provide an opportunity for each child to make choices during the day? Do the students feel that I value learning for both them and myself? Do I provide opportunities for each child to be successful? How do I link the value of the product, learning experience, or performance to what the child values? Does the product require the child to use the skill to show mastery?

_____

_____

_____

6. **Have I asked the parents or caregivers for more information?** Do they feel as though I value them as a resource and as partners? What can I do to help them feel comfortable enough to become a part of the learning community and classroom partner?

_____

_____

_____

7. **What member of the faculty do I respect and trust enough to ask questions when I am unsure of what to do?** Will this person be willing and available to meet with me frequently? Do we have similar teaching styles? Will we challenge and stimulate each other's teaching? Is there a mentor assigned to me (for new teachers or for teachers new to the grade level)?

_____

_____

_____

Once you have asked yourself the questions above and answered as fully as you can, go to the person you listed in question 7 and ask the following questions when needed.

Things to Ask a Colleague

1. **What are some teaching strategies that you use to help you analyze what is not working in the classroom?** What assessments do you use to measure student engagement, interest, performance, and need?

_____
_____
_____

2. **How do you know when the student has mastered a skill?** What do you do when he or she seems to have it one day, but not the next? How do you know what skills and developmental levels are needed before you move on to the next skill level? How do you pre-assess your students to know if they are ready for the content in the lesson? What do you do if there is a learning difficulty or delay? How do you provide opportunities for the children to assess their work? How do you provide feedback during the lesson? Can I come to you to seek advice regarding issues of students who are not being successful?

_____
_____
_____

3. **What behavior management techniques do you use to address this problem?** How do you manage daily routines? What do you do if there is a behavior issue? How do you know what learning opportunities to provide during centers? How do you differentiate the activities?

_____
_____
_____

4. **Can we talk about the standards and how they connect to developmentally appropriate practice?** Could I come and observe how your daily routine/ behavior management strategies/lesson content is presented? What suggestions could you give me to make this lesson more engaging and interesting for my students? What does this piece of student work tell you about the lesson? What can I do to motivate my students?

_____
_____
_____

5. **How do you build relationships with parents and caregivers?** How do you address issues with parents and caregivers?

_____

_____

_____

6. **Where can I go to learn more about the standards, materials, content, etc., I am to teach?** Where can I find resources to help me grow professionally? How do you document information about each child?

_____

_____

_____

Glossary

Attention-deficit/hyperactivity disorder (ADHD) refers to a condition that impairs a person's ability to focus and attend to tasks in developmentally appropriate ways and limits the ability to control impulses and off-task behaviors. Individuals are not always diagnosed with both parts of this condition which include decreased attention capabilities and hyperactivity. Some of the more common characteristics of children with this condition include: difficulty in maintaining attention and concentration (with topics and activities of interest being attended to for extended periods of time); developmentally inappropriate activity and impulsivity; and excessive fidgeting or restlessness. Symptoms of this disorder usually appear in situations where prolonged attention is necessary, such as instructional settings at school, at work, and in some social situations, but to varying degrees

Developmentally appropriate refers to teaching practices in early childhood classrooms that adhere to the maturational development of each child regardless of chronological age. This is at the core of the learning-centered kindergarten classroom and the instructional focus that teachers are encouraged to use. By using teaching strategies and practices that align with learner development, the child experiences success, and academic progress is accelerated.

Expectations are the age appropriate academic, social, emotional, and behavioral skills and concepts to be demonstrated by the students.

Gifted and talented refers to individuals who are capable of performing at a high level, who possess outstanding abilities, and who, in order to meet their potential, require a differentiated educational program. These demonstrated abilities can be in a single focused area or a combination of any of the following areas: general intellectual ability, academic aptitude, creative thinking, leadership qualities, visual and performing arts, or psychomotor abilities.

Individualized Educational Program is commonly referred to as an IEP, and public schools are mandated by the Individuals with Disabilities Education Act (IDEA) to develop an IEP for every child who meets criteria set by federal and state requirements to qualify for special education services. The IEP must be designed to provide the child with a Free Appropriate Public Education (FAPE) and refers both to the education program provided to the individual student as well as to the legal written document that describes the program. An IEP must (1) describe how the school will assess the student's disability or disabilities, (2) assess the general curriculum and how the disability affects the learning process for the student, and (3) develop a plan of success for the student including educational goals and objectives as well as accommodations in the least restrictive learning environment.

Learning-centered kindergarten classrooms focus upon the individual learning needs of all students including emotional, social, cultural, physical, and academic needs. Using research-based practices, the teacher creates a learning environment where every child learns, every day, regardless of ability—no exceptions. Teachers who focus upon learning-centered practices use instructional strategies that allow the mandated content standards and other knowledge and skills to be taught in ways that are meaningful, engaging, and appropriate for all the children in their classes.

Learning centers are areas in a classroom where students engage in activities to facilitate or enrich learning skills. Learning centers can be used as independent practice of skills previously taught or as an exploration of a new skill in a small group. These activities can be modified and adapted to simultaneously meet the needs of all students in the classroom. Learning centers also provide an excellent opportunity for the teacher to observe performance of students, engage in conversations about their learning, and help students make connections to the world around them.

Learning differences involve any aspect of an individuals' lifestyle, student learning style, ability, interest, or experience that can impede upon their academic success. A language-learning different child, for instance, could be defined as a child with average or above average intelligence, without physical impairment or primary emotional disturbance, who is at risk to fail when exposed to conventional school experiences. Language learning differences include dyslexia, attention-deficit hyperactivity disorder, dysgraphia and dysphasia, or a combination of these differences.

Learning disability is usually defined as a disorder—cognitive, neurological, or psychological—that can limit an individual's ability to learn by affecting the way in which he or she takes in, remembers, understands, or expresses information. New research shows that students who have learning disabilities but experience interventions, opportunities, and appropriate accommodations early can catch up with normally developing peers.

Procedures are the routines in place for the daily operations of class. They include how to move about the room, acceptable ways for getting the teacher's attention, acquiring and using materials, requesting going to the restroom, and all the other basic ways a classroom works.

Rewards are special privileges or treats the student earns.

Special needs refers to individuals whose emotional or physical disorders, age, a history of abuse, or other factors contribute to the individual being at risk of failure to succeed in an academic setting. Guidelines for classifying a child as special needs vary by state. Common special needs include: serious medical conditions, emotional and behavioral disorders, history of abuse or neglect, medical or genetic risk due to familial mental illness or parental substance abuse, lack of educational opportunity, and homelessness or prolonged stays in foster care.

Standardized tests are an assessment tool frequently employed to evaluate students' mastery of standards. The word "standardized" does not have any connection to the standards that the students are expected to master, but rather describes the standard, uniform format of the tests and of the conditions under which the tests are administered and scored.

Standards are expectations of what students should know and be able to do in a particular subject or at a particular grade level. When linked to a grade level, as in "kindergarten standards," the term indicates the specific knowledge and skills across all subject areas that a student should learn in that grade. When used in conjunction with a discipline, such as "mathematics standards," the term refers to the body of math knowledge and the set of math skills a student should learn in grades kindergarten through twelve. Nearly every state has adopted a set of standards in certain areas; these standards determine what is taught at each grade level in those subjects.

Standards-based education involves setting high standards, providing effective instruction that enables all students to achieve those standards, and assessing the students' mastery using assessments aligned with those standards. A standards-based approach can be implemented in any type of educational context and used on any scale from a single classroom to the state or national level.

Helpful Readings to Strengthen Your Knowledge Base

Key 1

French, M. (2004). *Can you really say no? Standards and good practices can work together*. Little Rock, AK: Southern Early Childhood Association.

Helm, H. H., & Beneke, S. (2003). *The power of projects: Meeting contemporary challenges in early childhood classrooms-strategies and solutions*. New York: Teachers College Press.

Seefeldt, C. (2005). *How to work with standards in the early childhood classroom*. New York: Teachers College Press.

Key 2

Gregory, G., & Chapman, C. (2002). *Differentiated instructional strategies: One size doesn't fit all*. Thousand Oaks, CA: Corwin Press.

Tileston, D. W. (2005). *Ten best teaching practices: How brain research, learning styles, and standards define teaching competencies*. Thousand Oaks, CA: Corwin Press.

Willis, J. (2007). *Brain-friendly strategies for the inclusion classroom*. Alexandria, VA: Association for Supervision and Curriculum Development.

Key 3

Johnson, N. L. (1992). *Thinking is the key*. Beavercreek, OH: Creative Learning Consultants, Inc.

Kingore, B. (2004). *Differentiation: Simplified, realistic, and effective*. Austin: Professional Associates Publishing.

Levine, Melvin D. (2002). *A mind at a time*. New York: Simon & Schuster.

McNairy, S., Glasgow, N., & Hicks, C. (2005). *What successful teachers do in inclusive classrooms: 60 research-based teaching strategies that help special learners succeed*. Thousand Oaks, CA: Corwin Press.

Polette, N. (1999). *Activities for any picture book*. Pieces of Learning. Beavercreek, OH: Creative Learning Consultants, Inc.

Key 4

Erwin, J. C. (2004). *The classroom of choice: Giving students what they need and getting what you want.* Alexandria, VA: Association for Supervision and Curriculum Development.

Richardson, K. (1999). *Developing number concepts: Counting, comparing, and pattern.* Parsippany, NJ: Dale Seymour Publications.

Wong, H. K., & Wong, R. T. (1993). *The first days of school: How to be an effective teacher.* Mountain View, CA: Harry Wong Publications.

Key 5

Rose, D., & Meyer, A. (2002). *Teaching every student in the digital age: Universal design for learning.* Alexandria, VA: Association for Supervision and Curriculum Development.

Key 6

Eggers-Pièrola, C. (2005). *Connections & commitments: Reflecting Latino values in early childhood programs.* Portsmouth, NH: Heinemann.

Gaitan, C. D. (2004). *Involving Latino families in schools: Raising student achievement through home-school partnerships.* Thousand Oaks, CA: Corwin Press.

Key 7

Keyser, J. (2006). *From parents to partners: Building a family-centered early childhood program.* St. Paul, MN: Redleaf Press.

Powers, J. (2005). *Parent-friendly early learning: Tips and strategies for working well with families.* St.Paul, MN: Redleaf Press.

Prior, J., & Gerard, M. R. (2007). *Family involvement in early childhood education: Research into practice.* Clifton Park, NY: Thompson Delmar Learning.

Key 8

Lee, E., Menkart, D., & Okazawa-Rey, M. (Eds.). (1998). *Beyond heroes and holidays: A practical guide to K-12 anti-racist, multicultural education and staff development.* Washington, DC: Network of Educators on the Americas.

Schlechty, P. C. (2002). *Working on the work: An action plan for teachers, principals, and superintendents.* San Francisco: Jossey-Bass.

References

American Academy of Pediatrics. (2004). *Caring for your baby and young child: Birth to age 5.* (Shelov, S., M.D, F.A.A. P., & Hannemann, R.E., M.D., F.A.A.P., Eds.). New York: Bantum Books.

American Academy of Pediatrics. (2007). *Developmental Milestones.* Retrieved December 27, 2007 , from http://www.aap.org

American Psychiatric Association. (1994). *Diagnostic and statistical manual of mental disorders* (4th ed.). Washington DC: Author.

American Psychiatric Association. (2000). *Diagnostic and statistical manual of mental disorders* (4th ed.). Washington, DC: Author.

Clements, D. H., Nastasi, B. K., & Swaminathan, S. (1993). Young children and computers: Crossroads and directions from research. *Young Children, 48*(2), 56–64.

Davis, B. (2006). *How to teach students who don't look like you: Culturally relevant teaching strategies.* Thousand Oaks, CA: Corwin Press.

Deasy, R.J. (Ed.). (2002). *Critical links: Learning in the arts and student academic and social development.* Washington, DC: The Arts Education Partnership. Retrieved August 15, 2005, from www.aep-arts.org

The Dole Five-a-day interactive Web Site. (2004). The Dole Food Company, Inc. Retrieved December 27, 2007, from: http://www.dole5aday.com

Dunn, R., Dunn, K., & Perrin, J. (1994). *Teaching young children through their individual learning styles K–2.* Boston, MA: Allyn & Bacon.

Edwards, C., Gandini, L. , & Forman, G. (Eds.). (1998). *The hundred languages of children: The Reggio Emilia approach advanced reflections.* (2nd Edition). Westport, CT: Ablex Publishing.

Game Goo: Learning that Sticks. (2001). Retrieved December 27, 2007 from Cognitive Concepts, Inc. Web Site: http://www.cogcon.com

Evertson, C. M., & Neal, K. W. (2005). Looking into learning-centered classrooms: Implications for classroom management. In B. Demarest (Ed.), *Benchmarks for excellence* Washington, DC: National Education Association.

Gaitan, C. D. (2004). *Involving Latino families in schools: Raising student achievement through home-school partnerships.* Thousand Oaks, CA: Corwin Press.

Goleman, D. (1995). *Emotional intelligence.* New York: Bantam Books.

Good, T.L., & Brophy, J.E. (2000). *Looking in classrooms.* (8th Edition). New York, NY: Addison Wesley Longman.

Gregory, G.H., & Chapman, C. (2002). *Differentiated instructional strategies: One size doesn't fit all*. Thousand Oaks, CA: Corwin Press.

Hatch, J. A. (2002). Accountability shovedown: Resisting the standards movement in early childhood education. *Phi Delta Kappan, 83 (6)*, 457–463.

Hart, B., & Risley, T.R. (1995). *Meaningful differences in the everyday experience of young American children*. Baltimore, MD: Brookes Publishing Company.

Healy, J.M. (1990). *Endangered minds: Why children don't think and what we can do about it*. New York, NY: Touchstone: Simon & Schuster.

Hubert, D., (1995). *Welcome to the Flat Stanley Project*. Retrieved September 25, 2007, from http://www.flatstanley.com

Lawrence-Lightfoot, S. (2003). *The essential conversation: What parents and teachers can learn from each other*. New York: Ballantine Books.

Lee, E., Menkart, D., & Okazawa-Rey, M. (Eds.). (1998). *Beyond heroes and holidays: A practical guide to K–12 anti-racist, multicultural education and staff development*. Washington, DC: Network of Educators on the Americas.

National Association for the Education of Young Children. (1997). *Developmentally appropriate practice in early childhood programs serving children from birth through age 8. A position statement of the National Association for the education of young children*. Washington, DC: Author.

The National Autism Association. (n.d.). *All About Autism*. Retrieved October 15, 2007 from http://www.nationalautismassociation.org

Payne, R. K. (2002). *Understanding learning: The how, the why, the what*. Highlands, TX: Aha! Process.

Planet Interactive, Inc.Web site. (2007). Retrieved February 25, 2008, from www.learningplanet.com

Powers, J. (2005). *Parent-friendly early learning: Tips and strategies for working well with families*. St.Paul, MN: Redleaf Press.

Prior, J., & Gerard, M.R. (2007). *Family involvement in early childhood education: Research into practice*. Clifton Park, NY: Thompson Delmar Learning.

Schlechty, P. C. (2002). *Working on the work: An action plan for teachers, principals, and superintendents*. San Francisco, CA: Jossey-Bass.

Seefeldt, C. & Wasik, B. (2002). *Kindergarten: fours and fives go to school*. New Jersey: Merrill Prentice Hall.

Starfall.com Web site. (2007). Retrieved December 27, 2007 from http://www.starfall.com

Sternberg, R. (1996). *Successful intelligence: How practical and creative intelligence determine success in life*. New York: Simon & Schuster.

Willis, J. (2007). *Brain-friendly strategies for the inclusion classroom*. Alexandria, VA: Association for Supervision and Curriculum Development.

Wong, H.K., & Wong, R.T. (1993). *The first days of school: How to be an effective teacher*. Mountain View, CA: Harry Wong Publications.

All the clip art in the book can be found at http://www.clipart.com
Educational quotes used in this book are located at the following sites:
http://www.leading-learning.co.nz/famous-quotes.html
http://drwilliampmartin.tripod.com/bigedlist.htm

Index

CORWIN PRESS

The Corwin Press logo—a raven striding across an open book—represents the union of courage and learning. Corwin Press is committed to improving education for all learners by publishing books and other professional development resources for those serving the field of PreK–12 education. By providing practical, hands-on materials, Corwin Press continues to carry out the promise of its motto: **"Helping Educators Do Their Work Better."**